Arizona  BY THEME
DAY TRIPS

Leigh Wilson

Adventure Publications
Cambridge, Minnesota

Dedication

For Amy, Jenny, and Olivia, thanks for tagging along on my first-ever trip to Arizona way back in 2008! Love you guys!

Acknowledgments

For itinerary help and recommendations, thanks to Jackie Leatherman of Go Lake Havasu, Ann Steward of Visit Prescott, and Meg Roederer of Discover Flagstaff. For recommendations on Native Arizona, thanks go to Donovan Hanley of Detours Native America.

Safety Note Arizona is home to a variety of potentially dangerous animals, including venomous snakes, scorpions, as well as natural hazards, such as temperature extremes, sudden flash floods, and cliffs and dropoffs. Always heed posted safety warnings, take common-sense safety precautions, and remain aware of your surroundings. You're responsible for your own safety.

Cover and book design by Jonathan Norberg

Front cover photo: Wupatki National Monument (photographed by **Traveller70/Shutterstock.com**)

Back cover photo: Hot air balloons over London Bridge (photographed by **Angel McNall Photography /Shutterstock.com**)

All photos by Leigh Wilson, except pg. 4: **Chantal de Bruijne/shutterstock.com**; pg. 13: **Germany Feng/Shutterstock.com**; pg. 17: **Jim Parkin/shutterstock.com**; pg. 47: **Christopher Boswell/Shutterstock.com**; pg. 91: **BlaineT/Shutterstock.com**; pg. 126: **Travis Deyoe/Mount Lemmon SkyCenter/Steward Observatory**; pg. 139: **Jim Parkin/shutterstock.com**

10 9 8 7 6 5 4 3 2

Arizona Day Trips by Theme
Copyright © 2020 by Leigh Wilson
Published by Adventure Publications
An imprint of AdventureKEEN
310 Garfield Street South
Cambridge, Minnesota 55008
(800) 678-7006
www.adventurepublications.net
All rights reserved
Printed in China
ISBN 978-1-59193-889-7 (pbk.), ISBN 978-1-59193-890-3 (ebook)

Disclaimer Please note that travel information changes under the impact of many factors that influence the travel industry. We therefore suggest that you call ahead for confirmation when making your travel plans. Every effort has been made to ensure the accuracy of information throughout this book, and the contents of this publication are believed to be correct at the time of printing. Nevertheless, the publishers cannot accept responsibility for errors or omissions, for changes in details given in this guide, or for the consequences of any reliance on the information provided by the same. Assessments of attractions and so forth are based upon the author's own experiences; therefore, descriptions given in this guide necessarily contain an element of subjective opinion, which may not reflect the publisher's opinion or dictate a reader's own experience on another occasion.

Table of Contents

Arizona is a bright, dazzling place, and so is its artistic style

WHILE IT'S TRUE that Phoenix is home to the majority of fine arts and performance spaces in Arizona, there's art and culture to be had in every corner of the state. From Native American art to contemporary art and performing arts, this is a sampling of some of the work that Arizona artists are producing.

CULTURAL PURSUITS:
Performing & Visual Arts

Phoenix Art Museum, Phoenix, AZ

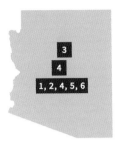

1 Arizona Opera

1636 N. Central Ave., Phoenix, AZ 85004; 602-266-7464, 520-293-4336
azopera.org

The Arizona Opera was born from the Tucson Opera Company, which was founded in 1971. Operas, concerts, and collaborative programs are produced throughout the state. The season includes five full-scale operas each year, with performances in Phoenix and Tucson as well as touring programs statewide. The season runs from September through April, and single-performance tickets start at a very reasonable $25.

2 Ballet Arizona

2835 E. Washington St., Phoenix, AZ 85034; 602-381-0184
balletaz.org

Entertaining Arizona audiences since 1986, Ballet Arizona is led by Ib Andersen, an alumnus of the New York City Ballet. The season kicks off in September with **Ballet Under the Stars,** a series of free performances at Phoenix-area parks and ends with summer evenings at the Desert Botanical Garden (see page 113) in May and June. The company also has a robust offering of classes for all ages through the School of Ballet Arizona.

3 Coconino Center for the Arts

2300 N. Fort Valley Road, Flagstaff, AZ 86001; 928-779-2300

Run by the Flagstaff Arts Council, the Coconino Center for the Arts is the hub of Flagstaff's vibrant arts and sciences community. This performing arts center and exhibition space has several gallery spaces featuring contemporary art and fine crafts. A 200-seat theater presents a wide variety of performances. Admission to the galleries is free, with donations accepted. Check the website for current exhibitions, which rotate frequently.

4 Cosanti and Arcosanti

Cosanti: 6433 E. Doubletree Ranch Road, Paradise Valley, AZ 85253; 480-948-6145
Arcosanti: Arcosanti Road, Mayer, AZ 86333; 928-632-7135
cosanti.com

Italian architect Paolo Soleri came to Arizona in the 1940s to study under Frank Lloyd Wright at Taliesin West, and he later became famous for his bronze and ceramic windbells. Cosanti is more than just an art gallery; you can watch live demonstrations at the foundry or take a guided tour of the property. Seventy miles north in the town of Mayer, Soleri founded Arcosanti, an ongoing experiment in urban architecture and environmental accountability. Tours are conducted daily, and there's a cafe on-site for lunch. It's an interesting stop if you're en route to Flagstaff or Prescott.

5 Mesa Arts Center

1 E. Main St., Mesa, AZ 85201; 480-644-6560
mesaartscenter.com

Downtown Mesa has an impressive performing and visual-arts campus, the largest in the state of Arizona. The **Mesa Contemporary Arts Museum** features four exhibits that rotate quarterly and spotlight artists from Arizona. The campus also has four theaters and more than a dozen art studios. A robust class calendar includes music, ceramics, photography, glass, sculpture, and much more. Free campus tours take place Wednesdays, September–May; private tours can be arranged with two weeks' notice.

6 Musical Instrument Museum

4725 E. Mayo Blvd., Phoenix, AZ 85050; 480-478-6000
mim.org

Often rated as one of the top attractions in Phoenix, the Musical Instrument Museum (MIM) is so much more than the name implies. Founded by Robert Ulrich, chairman emeritus of Target, to share his love of African instruments, MIM has more than 6,800 instruments on display from 200 countries and territories around the world. The gorgeous building flows naturally through each region of the world with engaging displays. Museum admission includes a wireless headset that plays automatically when you approach a display. The **Experience Gallery** allows guests to play instruments from around the world, while the **Artist Gallery** features instruments and apparel from music icons like Johnny Cash, Maroon 5, the Black Eyed Peas, Carlos Santana, and John Denver, just to name a few. Plan to spend at least a couple of hours exploring the galleries, café, and gift shop.

7 Phippen Museum

4701 AZ 89 N., Prescott, AZ 86301; 928-778-1385
phippenartmuseum.org

Prescott's Phippen Museum was founded by a Western painter and sculptor, George Phippen, who also founded the Cowboy Artists of America. This art gallery–cum–museum hosts a variety of rotating and permanent exhibits, including the **Arizona Rancher and Cowboy Hall of Fame.** A showcase of art and heritage of the American West, the museum contains sculptures and paintings depicting cowboys, American Indians, and impressive landscapes. The museum also has an expansive calendar of events and educational classes, plus a membership program which is part of the North American Reciprocal Museum Association, granting access to nearly 900 other museums.

8 Phoenix Art Museum

1625 N. Central Ave., Phoenix, AZ 85004; 602-257-1880
phxart.org

The Phoenix Art Museum has an impressive collection of art, ranging from Renaissance paintings to contemporary art, and it is the Southwest's largest art museum. The museum collection spans seven categories of art throughout the nearly 300,000 square feet of space. Collections include American, Asian, Contemporary, European, Fashion, Latin American, Modern, Photography, and Western American. Dozens of interesting exhibitions rotate frequently, such as the "Black Cloud" of 25,000 paper moths and butterflies at the museum entrance. There's an on-site restaurant, **Palette,** along with a well-curated gift shop. Outdoor spaces include cactus gardens and a sculpture garden. Closed on Mondays, the museum offers several free admission options, including Wednesdays after 3 p.m. and First Fridays. Art lovers can easily spend the better part of a day here, so plan accordingly!

9 Phoenix Theatre Company

1825 N. Central Ave., Phoenix, AZ, 85004; 602-254-2151
phoenixtheatre.com

Producing more than 400 performances a year, the Phoenix Theatre Company is the largest regional theatre company in the Valley of the Sun. Located next to the Phoenix Art Museum, it offers free parking, and you can grab a bite to eat beforehand at Palette (see previous page). The theatre has several stages as well as a lobby bar and bistro. The performance spaces were thoughtfully designed to ensure great seats for all. Enjoy performances of musicals such as *Jersey Boys* and *Kinky Boots*, along with spoofs like *Spamilton*, a parody of the musical *Hamilton*.

10 Scottsdale Arts

7380 E. Second St., Scottsdale, AZ 85251; 480-499-8587
scottsdalearts.org

The recently formed Scottsdale Arts organization consists of four branches: the **Scottsdale Center for the Performing Arts**, the **Scottsdale Museum of Contemporary Art**, **Scottsdale Public Art**, and **Scottsdale Arts Education & Outreach.** The Center for the Performing Arts hosts live music concerts, dance performances, film screenings, Broadway musicals, and more. Next door, the Museum of Contemporary Art presents contemporary art and architecture through interactive and immersive exhibits that engage your senses of sight and sound; exhibits rotate frequently, so there's always something new to explore. Scottsdale Public Art has created a free bicycle tour of several engaging outdoor art pieces throughout the city, including sculptures, light installations, and murals.

11 Tucson Desert Art Museum and Four Corners Gallery

7000 E. Tanque Verde Road, Tucson, AZ 85715; 520-202-3888
tucsondart.org

As much a history museum as an art museum, the Tucson Desert Art Museum focuses heavily on Native American art. An extensive exhibit on Navajo weaving tells the story of the mythical Spider Woman, while a past photography exhibit recounted Japanese evacuation and internment in Arizona during World War II. Other interesting exhibitions include clips and stills from Hollywood movies filmed in Tucson and other parts of Arizona, as well as an exhibit on contemporary Native American female art. The Four Corners Gallery next door features local

12, 13

artists with Southwest themes, while the museum store sells hand-crafted jewelry, pottery, and ceramics, among other gift items. Open Wednesday–Sunday, the museum is closed during July and August, as well as on all major holidays.

12 Tucson Museum of Art and Historic Block

140 N. Main Ave., Tucson, AZ 85701; 520-624-2333
tucsonmuseumofart.org

The Tucson Museum of Art campus in Tucson's Presidio neighborhood encompasses five Sonoran row houses listed on the National Register of Historic Places (one of these, the **Fish House,** is among Tucson's oldest homes, dating to 1868). The museum collections encompass Western, modern, and contemporary art, along with the longest-running statewide juried exhibition of Arizona artists. Daily tours are included in the price of admission, while private docent-led tours can be arranged by appointment. First Thursdays offer free admission from 5 p.m. to 8 p.m., with a cash bar and live performances each month. Attached to the museum is **Café a la C'art,** serving refined American entrées in the 1865 Hiram Stevens adobe. The museum is closed on Mondays.

13 University of Arizona Museum of Art

1031 Olive Road, Tucson, AZ 85721; 520-621-7567
artmuseum.arizona.edu

Of the many museums to explore on the University of Arizona campus, the Museum of Art is on the smaller side, but it has some impressive art worth viewing. This museum is perhaps best known today for the Willem de Kooning painting that was stolen in 1985 and recovered in 2017 through an estate sale; the painting is expected to be repaired and returned to the museum in the summer of 2020. Other impressive pieces include work by Jackson Pollock, Georgia O'Keeffe, and Norman Rockwell. One of the most popular works at the museum is a 15th-century Spanish altarpiece from a cathedral in Ciudad Rodrigo. The museum is closed on Mondays and university holidays.

Mesa Arts Center, Mesa, AZ

Monument Valley Navajo Tribal Park, Kayenta, AZ

ARIZONA AMERICAN INDIAN HISTORY and culture, which pre-dates the arrival of Spaniards and Americans by thousands of years, is an integral part of Arizona history. The sites listed in this chapter are of particular importance to Arizona's Indians and are highly recommended to anyone wanting to learn about the state's various indigenous cultures. *Note:* The Navajo Nation observes daylight saving time, while the rest of Arizona does not, so pay close attention to operating hours, and call ahead if you're unsure.

ARIZONA HISTORY:

American Indian History & Culture

Native American dancers at a Powwow in Arizona

1 Amerind Museum & Art Gallery

2100 N. Amerind Road, Dragoon, AZ 85609; 520-586-3666
amerind.org

A hidden gem just off I-10 between Tucson and Willcox, the Amerind Museum houses one of the best privately maintained collections of Native American art and artifacts from all over the Western Hemisphere. The museum, founded by archeologist William Fulton in 1937, "seeks to foster and promote knowledge and understanding of Native Peoples of the Americas through research, education, and conservation." The Main Gallery features the exhibit *A Century of Zuni and Navajo Jewelry*. The Ethnology Room has an interesting exhibit on the importance of running in Native tribes, from ancient times to today. Another large exhibit presents the history of Paquimé, an ancient ruin in Chihuahua, Mexico. A great roster of special events includes an annual tamale-making class and regular musical and dance performances. Closed Mondays and major holidays.

2 Elden Pueblo Archaeological Site

US 89 North (1 mile north of Flagstaff Mall), Flagstaff, AZ; 928-526-0866 or 928-699-5421
fs.usda.gov/recarea/coconino/recarea/?recid=55092

In the shadow of Mount Elden, on the north side of Flagstaff, this archaeological site has a small parking lot and pamphlets available for a self-guided tour. It's estimated that up to 200 Sinagua people lived here sometime between AD 1150 and AD 1250. Fifteen numbered posts along the 0.5-mile trail explain the various ruins and building techniques as you view the footprints that are left where 60–80 rooms once stood. While Elden Pueblo isn't as well preserved as other ruins in Arizona, it's a nice place for an educational walk in the woods.

3 Heard Museum

2301 N. Central Ave., Phoenix, AZ 85004; 602-252-8840
heard.org

Founded in 1929, the Heard Museum has become the world's preeminent museum for the presentation, interpretation, and advancement of American Indian art. Even the grounds of the building are remarkable. Free daily guided tours give you a great introduction to the museum and the integral role of Native cultures in Arizona history. The guided tour will walk you through several rooms representing various tribes and eras of Native history in Arizona and beyond. The exhibit *Home: Native People in the Southwest* showcases artifacts from ancestral Pueblo, Zuni, Hopi, Acuna, and Navajo peoples. The exhibit also incorporates a large collection of Katsina dolls, including more than 400 donated by former Senator Barry Goldwater. Check the website for special events and exhibits.

4 Homolovi State Park

AZ 87, Winslow, AZ 86047; 928-289-4106
azstateparks.com/homolovi

This state park near Winslow protects ancient ancestral sites of the Hopi people. The park was created in 1986 with the cooperation of the Hopi people. There are two main archaeology sites, **Homolovi I** and **Homolovi II,** the latter pueblo containing an estimated 1,200–2,000 rooms. Three trails provide just over 2 miles of hiking, with several points of interest including milling points and petroglyphs. The park also has a small campground, visitor center, and gift shop. Although the park is open to the public, the land is considered sacred by the Hopi; please keep this in mind when visiting.

5 Hopi Cultural Center

AZ 264 just north of Indian Route 4, Second Mesa, AZ 86043; 928-734-2401
hopiculturalcenter.com

Though the Hopi Reservation is located entirely within the Navajo Nation, just east of Tuba City and spread across 12 villages on three mesas, Hopi culture is very different from that of the Navajo. Begin your visit to the Hopi lands at the Cultural Center on the Second Mesa, comprising a museum, several shops, a hotel, and a restaurant. You can also hire a tour guide here to visit other areas of the mesas. **Old Oraibi** on the Third Mesa is believed to be the oldest continuously inhabited settlement in the United States. Some Hopi events, such as Katsina dances, are open to the public. In general, photography, recording, and sketching on-site are prohibited—please check with someone at the hotel or museum if you're unsure.

6 Hubbell Trading Post National Historic Site

One-half mile west of US 191, Ganado, AZ 86505; 928-755-3475
nps.gov/hutr

Trading posts were an important part of Native American culture—traders provided supplies to tribes who saw their lifestyles changing as the US expanded westward. John Lorenzo Hubbell began trading here

in 1876, as the Navajo people struggled to adjust to reservation life following the 1864 Long Walk. Hubbell's trading post became their liaison to the outside world, and even served as a makeshift hospital when smallpox hit the reservation in 1886. Hubbell Trading Post stayed in the family until 1967, when it was turned over to the National Park Service for preservation. The trading post still sells authentic American Indian rugs, jewelry, pottery and baskets, along with snacks, drinks, and souvenirs. In addition to the trading post, a visitor center explains the history of the area; there are also live weaving demonstrations and a bookstore.

7 Monument Valley Navajo Tribal Park

Indian Route 42, Olijato–Monument Valley, AZ 84536; 435-727-5870
monumentvalleytours.com

One of the Southwest's iconic landscapes, Monument Valley straddles the Utah–Arizona border near the Four Corners area. In the 1930s Hollywood director John Ford "discovered" Monument Valley and subsequently filmed several movies here. More recently, films like *Easy Rider* and *Forrest Gump* have imprinted the monuments onto American film history. Monument Valley, managed by the Navajo Nation, remains largely untouched, with only a dirt road circling the sandstone monuments, including the famed Mitten Buttes. Private vehicles are allowed on the 17-mile loop road, which is suitable for passenger vehicles in good weather. Many tours are offered, including several that visit areas otherwise restricted to visitors. Nearby facilities include **The View Hotel** inside the park and **Goulding's Trading Post and Lodge** just outside.

8 Navajo Code Talkers Museum

10 Main St., Tuba City, AZ 86045; 928-283-5441
discovernavajo.com/museums.aspx

Despite American Indians not earning the right to vote in all states until 1962, an estimated 99% of all eligible Natives had registered for the draft in 1942. The Navajo role in World War II and the development of their unique code—the only unbroken code language in the history of warfare—are an underreported phenomenon of the era.

This small, free museum screens a 50-minute movie that educates visitors about the language before they tour the exhibits. The displays include several uniforms and photos from WWII. If you travel to Monument Valley, the **Burger King** on US 160 in Kayenta also has a nice display dedicated to the Navajo code talkers inside.

9 Navajo Interactive Museum

10 Main St., Tuba City, AZ 86045; 928-640-0684
discovernavajo.com/museums.aspx

Originally opened as part of the 2002 Winter Olympics in Salt Lake City, this museum sits just behind the Tuba City Trading Post and the Navajo Code Talkers Museum (see above), making it easy to explore all three attractions at the same time. Your visit starts with a short video that explains the four worlds that the Diné (Navajo) have passed through to the present day and explains the symbolism of the four directions. As you then enter the museum, you follow along on the Navajo life journey through each of the directions. The museum also includes a model hogan and a small gift shop.

10 Navajo National Monument

End of AZ 564 (about 9 miles north of US 160), Shonto, AZ; 928-672-2700
nps.gov/nava

This National Monument was created to protect three ancestral Puebloan villages located in Tsegi Canyon. Like many other Arizona ruins, these villages were used from around AD 1250 to AD 1300. You can view the cliff dwellings of Betatkin from a short trail at the visitor center, but for a close-up look you'll need to join a free ranger-led tour to the site. Tours are offered daily, May–mid-October, and depart each morning at 8:15 and 10 a.m. A visit to the **Keet Seel** ruins (May–October only) requires a 17-mile hike; often done as an overnight, it requires a permit and mandatory orientation meeting the day before your hike.

11 Navajo Nation Museum & Visitor's Center

AZ 264 at Window Rock Loop Road, Window Rock, AZ 86515; 928-871-7941
discovernavajo.com/museums.aspx

Window Rock is the capital of the Navajo Nation, and the buildings here are the seat of tribal government. The main building housing the Navajo Nation Museum & Visitor's Center is shaped like a large hogan. The Visitor's Center, a great place to begin your visit to the Navajo Nation, has a bookstore, gift shop, snack bar, auditorium, and library. The museum includes art, artifacts, and interpretive displays.

12

13 Various locations

Elsewhere in Window Rock, you can also visit **Window Rock Tribal Park** (about 0.1 mile north of Indian Route 100; 928-871-6647), which has a statue commemorating the code talkers, as well as the **Navajo Nation Zoo and Botanical Park** (34 AZ 264; 928-871-6574, navajozoo.org

12 Pueblo Grande Museum

4619 E. Washington St., Phoenix, AZ 85034; 602-495-0901
phoenix.gov/parks/arts-culture-history/pueblo-grande

In the shadow of Sky Harbor International Airport, Pueblo Grande Museum has preserved one of the largest Hohokam villages; it once housed more than 1,000 people. The museum and archaeological park include several indoor exhibits, an outdoor trail, and a gift shop. Start inside with a 10-minute movie that provides some history of the Hohokam, who were known for irrigation, engineering, and agriculture. The Hohokam canals, among the most sophisticated irrigation networks ever created, once supported up to 50,000 people. The outside trail is 0.66 mile long and weaves through excavated ruins of the village, including an ancient ball court. Groups can register in advance for a docent-led tour; monthly tours of the ancient canals are also available. Check the website for special events and exhibits throughout the year. Another urban ruins site is **Mesa Grande Cultural Park,** just 9 miles east in Mesa (1000 N. Date St.; 480-644-3075, arizonamuseumofnaturalhistory.org).

13 Powwows

Statewide; check calendar.powwows.com for more information

Powwows are a wonderful way to experience Native culture and celebrations, and they're among the few traditional ceremonies that are open to the public. A number of these events are held throughout the state, with nearly continuous daytime and evening performances. Various drums provide music for the dancers. The "tiny tots" pow wows are darling, and even spectators are allowed to join the dancing at certain times during the ceremony. There are usually vendors selling food, drinks, jewelry, clothing, and gifts. Bring a chair and umbrella for daytime shade, warm layers for the evening, and cash for parking and food. If a handout of guidelines isn't provided, feel free to ask for guidance on photography and recording—don't assume it's OK to take video or pictures without checking first.

Here's a partial list of powwows held in Arizona throughout the year.

MARCH

Apache Gold Casino Resort Intertribal Pow Wow
San Carlos Event Center, 5 US Hwy 70, San Carlos, AZ 85550

Wa:k Pow Wow
Mission San Xavier del Bac, 1950 W. San Xavier Road, Tucson, AZ 85746

APRIL

Flagstaff Healing & Wellness Pow Wow
Northern Arizona University Fieldhouse, 1050 S. Knoles Drive, Flagstaff, AZ 86001

Pow Wow at Arizona State University
Sun Devil Football Stadium, 500 E. Veterans Way, Tempe, AZ 85287

AUGUST

Thunder Mountain Pow Wow
Kaibab Paiute Indian Reservation, AZ 389A at Pipe Springs Road, Fredonia, AZ 86022

SEPTEMBER

Prescott Social Intertribal Pow Wow
Watson Lake Park, 3101 Watson Lake Park Road, Prescott, AZ 86301

OCTOBER

Roy Track Memorial Mesa Pow Wow
Mesa Riverview Park, 2100 W. Rio Salado Parkway, Mesa, AZ 85201

NOVEMBER

Red Mountain Eagle Pow Wow
Salt River Pima-Maricopa Community Baseball Field, 1839 N. Longmore Road, Scottsdale, AZ 85256

DECEMBER

Shonto New Year's Pow Wow
Shonto Preparatory School Gymnasium, US 160 at AZ 98, Shonto, AZ 86054

Mammoth Steakhouse & Saloon, Goldfield, AZ

THOUGHTS OF ARIZONA evoke images of the Wild West, and Western culture is indeed evident throughout the state. From gold rush outposts and Mexican–Indian wars to rodeos that still draw crowds, it's not difficult to catch a glimpse of the Wild West in these ghost towns and attractions. All of the towns listed here are accessible with a regular passenger vehicle, although dirt roads may not be passable after recent rains. This is just a small sampling of the ghost towns in Arizona; there are more than 40 ghost towns and mining camps in the Bradshaw Mountains alone.

ARIZONA HISTORY:
Ghost Towns & the Wild West

25

1 Castle Dome City

Castle Dome Mine Road, Yuma, AZ; 928-920-3062
castledomemuseum.org

Silver was mined in Castle Dome, 45 miles north of Yuma, from 1864 until 1979, making it the longest worked mining district in Arizona. The site is now privately owned and operated as the Castle Dome Museum & Ghost Town. There are more than 50 buildings to explore; 7 are original, and the rest have been rebuilt using materials found around the ghost town. The owners have extensively explored over 300 mines in the area, pulling out artifacts for the museum. Reenactors perform daily in the high season (October 15–April 15). The ghost town and museum are also open during the summer, but call ahead as hours vary.

2 Cochise County Ghost Town Trail

Cochise County, AZ

Cochise County in southeast Arizona has several ghost towns, many of which can be strung together for a nice auto tour ending in the famous Wild West town of **Tombstone.** You start in **Pearce,** which was a wealthy town in the early 20th century thanks to local silver and gold mines; it boasted hotels, swimming pools, and automobiles. Today, you can visit the Pearce Jail and the Pearce Cemetery, where Abraham Lincoln's bodyguard, George Hart Platt, is buried. Next along the trail is **Courtland,** which once had 23 mines and a population of 2,000 who were served by two railroad lines. Trains stopped serving the town in 1938, however, and all that remains today are a few building hulls. My favorite stop on this route is the ghost town of **Gleeson,** which prospered until the 1930s; today, a former resident mans the Gleeson Jail, which is now a museum. From Gleeson it's just a few miles down the road to Tombstone. Although the nearby town of **Cochise** isn't a ghost town, you can visit or stay at the **Cochise Hotel** (5062 N. Cochise Stronghold Road; 818-480-8047, cochisehotel.net), which dates to 1882 and is now on the National Register of Historic Places.

3 | Frontier Town

6245 E. Cave Creek Road, Cave Creek, AZ 85331; 480-488-9129
frontiertown.info

Revisit the Wild West at Frontier Town in Cave Creek, about an hour north of Phoenix. Roam wooden sidewalks lined with old-timey shops, attractions, and a haunted cemetery. The shops carry regional items like salsas and prickly pear candy, along with Western-themed clothing and home decor. Although Frontier Town more closely resembles a ghost town in the heat of summer, winter visitors will be treated to stunt shows, shootouts, and special events. The **Silver Spur Saloon & Restaurant** is expected to reopen soon following a 2016 fire.

4 | Goldfield Ghost Town

4650 N. Mammoth Mine Road, Apache Junction, AZ 85119; 480-983-0333
goldfieldghosttown.com

Set against the scenic backdrop of the Superstition Mountains east of Phoenix, Goldfield is an old mining town repurposed into a Wild West–themed attraction. In the 1890s, Goldfield was booming, but the glory days lasted less than a decade, and it became a ghost town in 1898, with all of the buildings eventually crumbling. The site was purchased and rebuilt in the 1980s, and today it boasts the only operational narrow-gauge railroad in Arizona. There are so many things to do in Goldfield that you can easily spend a full day or more here; choose from mine tours, jeep tours, train rides, an old-time photo studio, a shooting gallery, and a zip line. There are plenty of food options, too, including a bakery, an ice-cream parlor, and a snack bar.

5 | Jerome

Jerome, AZ, 86331; 928-634-1066
jeromechamber.com

The not-quite-ghost-town of Jerome was once called the "Wickedest Town in the West" and produced more than $1 billion in copper, gold, and silver. The town itself seems to defy gravity, clinging to the side of Mingus Mountain. The main road through town switchbacks down the hill past bars, art galleries, boutiques, and restaurants. Although today's population of 450 is much less than the 15,000 who once lived here, Jerome is still very much a living town with local residents. However, they take the ghost town moniker quite seriously, and ghost tours are a popular activity in Jerome. You can learn more about the mining history of Jerome at nearby **Jerome State Historic Park** (100 Douglas Road; 928-634-5381, azstateparks.com/jerome) and the **Jerome Mine Museum** in town (200 Main St.; 928-634-5477, jeromehistoricalsociety.com/museums-buildings/mine-museum).

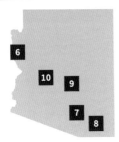

6 Oatman

Oatman, AZ 86433; 928-768-6222
oatmangoldroad.org

In the Black Mountains, just 14 miles east of the Colorado River and the California border, lies the ghost town of Oatman. Founded in the early 1900s, Oatman hit it big in 1915 when prospectors struck $10 million in gold. Fame fizzled fast for Oatman, however, as the gold ran out; then Route 66 was moved 20 miles south to I-40 in the 1960s. The main draw to Oatman today is the pack of wild burros that still roam the town, descended from burros brought in during the gold-mining days. Visitors can purchase food for the burros in most of the shops in town. Many buildings in Oatman are original, now housing souvenir shops selling jewelry, moccasins, T-shirts, and cold drinks. Actors stage shootouts on the main strip, and tour buses can arrange to be "held up" by bandits as they pass through town.

7 Old Tucson

201 Kinney Road, Tucson, AZ 85735; 520-883-0100
oldtucson.com

This 1860s Wild West town outside of Tucson was made for movies, but you'd never know the difference! The town was actually built in 1939 for Western films, and those buildings are still what you see today. In true Hollywood fashion, 50 buildings went up in 40 days, thanks in part to 100 Tohono O'odham who were hired to construct the adobe buildings. The first movie, *Arizona,* starring William Holden and Jean Arthur, filmed here in 1940, with hundreds of others following. Filming continues today, but the park is also open to the public, with limited hours in the summer. Catch a shootout at high noon, a stunt show, or a musical in the saloon. There's also plenty of shopping, along with a few cafés and stagecoach rides. It's fun to check out the list of films shot here and watch one before you visit.

8 Tombstone

Tombstone, AZ 85638; 888-457-3929
comevisittombstoneaz.com

Perhaps Arizona's most famous Wild West ghost town, Tombstone is the site of the world-famous gunfight at the O.K. Corral in 1881. The most famous shootout in the history of the American West lasted only 30 seconds, but Tombstone will forever be known as the "Town Too Tough to Die." Visitors today can experience live reenactments, daily shows, museums, and historical tours, and enjoy historic restaurants, saloons, and lodges. Many films have been shot here, including the 1993 movie *Tombstone,* starring Kurt Russell as Wyatt Earp. Stagecoach rides are offered through the town's main street. A visit to Tombstone is a great starting point for a tour of the ghost towns of **Cochise County** (see page 26) or a nice rest stop on your way to the historic mining town of **Bisbee.**

9 Tortilla Flat

Tortilla Flat, AZ 85190; 480-984-1776
tortillaflataz.com

Arizona's smallest official community, Tortilla Flat is the last surviving stagecoach stop on the Apache Trail. Located 18 miles past Apache Junction, this town (population: 6) has been serving weary travelers since 1904. What remains today is the **Superstition Saloon & Restaurant,** the **Tortilla Flat General Store and Ice Cream Shop,** the **Mercantile & Gift Shop,** and the **Tortilla Flat Post Office.** The Superstition Saloon boasts live music every day between Christmas and Easter. This is a popular stop between Phoenix and Canyon Lake, so be prepared for crowds on summer weekends.

10 Vulture City

36610 355th Ave., Wickenburg, AZ 85390; 877-425-9229
vultureminetours.com

While most of Arizona is known for copper mining, the Vulture Mine was the most successful gold mine in the state. As many as 5,000 people lived here at the town's peak until war efforts closed the mine in 1942. Today, several buildings remain in what is absolutely a true ghost town. Tour the post office, a brothel, the cookhouse, and many other buildings that give you a tiny glimpse into frontier life of the late 19th century. Touring the site requires a fee that can be prepaid online. (That's right—even ghost towns aren't immune to e-commerce!) While Vulture City is open year-round, it's best to visit on a weekend between late October and mid-May, when guided tours are given.

11 Whiskey Row

North Montezuma Street, Prescott, AZ 86301
prescott.com/whiskey-row

Prescott is one of my favorite towns in Arizona, and Whiskey Row is where it all began. This one block of Montezuma Street once held 40 bars, conveniently facing the courthouse on the town square. While Prescott isn't as wild as it once was, it's still fun to take a stroll down Whiskey Row, although you're just as likely to hit up an ice-cream parlor as a pub. **The Palace** (120 S. Montezuma St.; 928-541-1996, whiskeyrowpalace.com) opened in 1877, is one of the oldest bars in Arizona; it retains that saloon atmosphere right down to the wait-staff's uniforms. Whiskey Row also happens to be the hub of Prescott's many special events, including the Christmas courthouse lighting and classic-car shows.

Wild Burros of Oatman, AZ

Mission San Xavier del Bac, Tucson, AZ

ARIZONA MAY LACK the Colonial history and cobblestone streets of the East Coast, but there's no shortage of historic buildings and structures here. From groundbreaking innovation to 18th-century Spanish missions to Frank Lloyd Wright creations, there are plenty of interesting sights for architecture and history fans visiting Arizona.

ARIZONA HISTORY:
Historic Buildings & Architecture

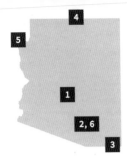

1 Arizona Biltmore

2400 E. Missouri Ave., Phoenix, AZ 85016; 602-955-6600
arizonabiltmore.com

Designed in the 1920s by Frank Lloyd Wright student Albert Chase McArthur, the Arizona Biltmore has been welcoming posh guests for nearly 100 years. Frank Lloyd Wright himself was a consultant on the building project, and the hotel was owned for a time by the Wrigley family as a private club for guests at their nearby mansion (see page 37). Once known as the "Jewel of the Desert," the Arizona Biltmore even hosted Ronald and Nancy Reagan on their honeymoon in 1952. Today, the hotel is a full-service resort that's part of the Waldorf Astoria family. History tours (complimentary for hotel guests) are given three times a week, and there's also a Happy Hour History tour on Fridays.

2 Fox Tucson Theatre

17 W. Congress St., Tucson, AZ 85701; 520-547-3040
foxtucson.com

Tucson's Fox Theatre opened in 1930 and is a gorgeous example of an Art Deco movie palace. For 40 years, the Fox was the grand dame of downtown Tucson, hosting movies, vaudeville shows, and concerts before falling into disrepair in the 1970s as commerce and entertainment moved to multiplexes and suburban shopping malls. Fortunately, in 1999 a nonprofit was formed to purchase and restore the Fox. They've done an amazing job of bringing the Fox back to its original glory and filling the calendar with fun performances. If you can't catch a performance, free tours are conducted on the second Tuesday of the month, from September through May.

3 The Gadsden Hotel

1046 G Ave., Douglas, AZ 85607; 520-364-4481
thegadsdenhotel.com

A working hotel on the National Register of Historic Places, The Gadsden Hotel holds an important place in Arizona history. The hotel originally opened in 1907 and, with the exception of a post-fire rebuild in 1928, has been in continuous operation. No expense was spared in the hotel, incorporating then-cutting-edge technology like an electric lift and a telephone switchboard. The Gadsden, still the hub of downtown Douglas, is undergoing renovations to modernize the facilities while maintaining the hotel's historic allure. If you aren't spending the night in Douglas, call ahead to schedule a tour ($10, by appointment only).

4 Glen Canyon Dam

Page, AZ
nps.gov/glca/planyourvisit/guidedtours.htm

It took only 20 years for demand to exceed the capacity of the Hoover Dam, so additional dams were needed along the Colorado River to supply electricity to the growing Southwest US population. Construction began, with much controversy from environmentalists, in 1956 and formed Lake Powell. Not coincidentally, this was the last great dam built in the West, as environmental groups pushed strongly to avoid future dams of this size. Probably the most famous opponent of the dam is author Edward Abbey, whose fictional *Monkey Wrench Gang* targeted the dam. Another great book on the topic is *The Emerald Mile,* which details a failure in the dam in the 1980s which released unprecedented water levels through the Grand Canyon. Today, up to seven guided tours are given each day by the Glen Canyon Conservancy.

5 Hoover Dam

Lake Mead, Nevada
usbr.gov/lc/hooverdam

One of the seven Industrial Wonders of the World, Hoover Dam was really ahead of its time when it was completed in 1936. The dam, which is more than 700 feet tall, was built in the Black Canyon of the Colorado River, along the Arizona–Nevada border. Hoover Dam generates enough power to serve more than one million residents in Arizona, Nevada, and California. Highway traffic from Nevada to Arizona passed right over the dam until 2010, when the Mike O'Callaghan–Pat Tillman Memorial Bridge opened, affording drivers a unique view of the dam. Hoover Dam tours are conducted every day except Thanksgiving and Christmas.

6 Mission San Xavier del Bac

1950 W. San Xavier Road, Tucson, AZ 85746; 520-294-2624
sanxaviermission.org

The original mission was founded here by Father Eusebio Francisco Kino in 1692 and named after St. Francis Xavier. The current building

was completed in 1797, making it the oldest intact European structure in Arizona. The mission sits in the village of Wa:k, in the Tohono O'odham Nation, and is still an active church today. Mass is held daily, and free docent-led tours are available when services aren't in progress. The site includes a small gift shop and a museum, and there's a nearby hill you can climb for aerial views of the mission. Bring cash for parking-lot vendors—this is a good place to try a fry-bread taco!

7 Navajo Bridge

US 89A, Marble Canyon, AZ; 928-355-2319
nps.gov/glca/learn/historyculture/navajobridge.htm

This beautiful span consists of two bridges over the Colorado River in Marble Canyon. The original 1929 Navajo Bridge replaced Lee's Ferry, which at the time was the only place to cross the Colorado River for miles in each direction. When the bridge was built, it was the highest steel-arch bridge in the world, and it joined the National Register of Historic Places in 1981. In the 1990s a newer bridge was constructed to keep pace with traffic and growing vehicle sizes, but great care was taken to ensure that the new bridge mirrors the old one. Today, the bridges remain side by side: one for pedestrians and one for vehicles. It's often possible to see peregrine falcons in the area around the bridge, and for river rafters setting off from Lee's Ferry, this is the last sign of civilization they will see for many miles until they reach Phantom Ranch in Grand Canyon National Park.

8 Taliesin West

12621 N. Frank Lloyd Wright Blvd., Scottsdale, AZ 85259; 480-627-5340
franklloydwright.org/taliesin-west

Blending into the surrounding McDowell Mountains is Scottsdale's only National Historic Landmark. Taliesin West was designed in 1937 by American architect Frank Lloyd Wright, the pioneer of the Prairie School of architecture. It's the winter home of the School of Architecture at Taliesin, formerly the Frank Lloyd Wright School of Architecture. Architecture students study here from October to May and then return to Taliesin in Wisconsin for the rest of the year. Seventy-five percent of Frank Lloyd Wright's designs were private homes, but Taliesin West is unique in that it includes living quarters, a dining hall and study area, and a kiva meeting space, plus public spaces, including multiple performance theaters. Tours and special events are held daily; reservations are strongly recommended. Taliesin West is closed on Tuesdays and Wednesdays from June through August.

9 Wrigley Mansion

2501 E. Telawa Trail, Phoenix, AZ 85016; 602-955-4079
wrigleymansion.com

Arizona has many Midwest connections, and the Wrigley family is a prominent one. William Wrigley Jr. made his fortune with chewing gum and subsequently built five mansions across the United States. Phoenix's Wrigley Mansion was built in 1930, adjacent to the Arizona Biltmore hotel (see page 34), which Wrigley also owned. Perched on a hill overlooking Phoenix and the surrounding mountain ranges, Wrigley Mansion is now operated as a wedding and event venue. Zoning laws require this to remain a private club, but a $5 trial membership (good for one month) can be purchased by one member of each visiting party. Historical tours are given several times per day, and several tour/lunch packages are offered, which include a meal at **Geordie's Restaurant** after the tour.

Tumacácori National Historic Park, Tumacácori, AZ

ALTHOUGH ARIZONA WAS THE LAST of the 48 contiguous states to join the Union, there is a rich history here that goes back for centuries. The Spanish first explored the region in the 16th century, followed by the establishment of the Catholic Mission San Xavier del Bac in 1692 and the Spanish fort at Tubac in 1752. After the Mexican War of Independence in 1812, Arizona became part of Mexico and remained so until the Gadsden Purchase in 1853. It would be another 59 years before Arizona became a US state.

ARIZONA HISTORY:
Historic Sites

1 Coronado National Memorial

4101 W. Montezuma Canyon Road, Hereford, AZ 85615; 520-366-5515
nps.gov/coro

If you're willing to get off the beaten path pretty close to the Mexico border, this memorial is all about the 16th-century Coronado expedition. In the first of many major disruptions to local Natives, Francisco Vázquez de Coronado came north in search of the Seven Cities of Gold. Start your visit at the visitor center to get an overview of the history of the expedition and the transformation of the border region over the years. There are several hiking trails at the memorial, and it's a great spot for spotting migratory birds. You can also explore **Coronado Cave,** but there are no guided tours—you must bring your own equipment, including lights and helmets.

2 Fort Bowie National Historic Site

3500 Apache Pass Road, Bowie, AZ 85605; 520-847-2500
nps.gov/fobo

Another remote historic site worth detouring for is the Fort Bowie National Historic Site. As the site is 8 miles down a dirt road (suitable for passenger cars), you'll want to leave plenty of time for both the drive and the 1.5-mile hike from the parking lot. The surrounding Chiricahua Mountains were ground zero for the Apache Indian wars, and this site provides an informative overview of the conflicts of the late 19th century. One of the more interesting spots is the **Fort Bowie Cemetery,** which has been painstakingly reconstructed. Soldiers, Mexicans, and Apaches were all buried here, including one of Geronimo's sons. Don't make the drive out here if you're unable to hike to the site—although there are interpretive signs along the way, this is not a typical historic site where the visitor center is located in the parking lot.

3 Fort Verde State Historic Park

125 E. Hollamon St., Camp Verde, AZ 86322; 928-567-3275
azstateparks.com/fort-verde

Just off I-17 between Phoenix and Flagstaff, Camp Verde was established in 1865 to protect European settlers from the Tonto-Apache and Yavapai Indians, who had been here for many years before the Arizona Territory was established. Many years after the fort was abandoned in 1891, the area became a state park in 1970 and restoration began on several buildings. Today, three of the homes are listed on the National Register of Historic Places and have been restored and furnished in late-19th-century style. In addition to interesting exhibits on Indian Scouts and Buffalo Soldiers, the park has a great roster of events, including living-history programs, candlelight tours, and a Victorian Christmas celebration.

4 Heritage Square

113 N. Sixth St., Phoenix, AZ 85004; 602-262-5070
heritagesquarephx.org

For a quiet break from the bustle of downtown Phoenix, Heritage Square is a nice respite and a fun place to spend an hour or two. I stumbled upon this square when visiting the nearby Arizona Science Center (see page 124). Built around the original townsite of Phoenix, the square has several points of interest. The **Rosson House** is a beautifully restored 1895 Victorian home that is open for guided tours Wednesday–Sunday. Other historic buildings in the square have been repurposed as gift shops, antique stores, a coffee shop, and the award-winning **Pizzeria Bianco,** which is housed in a former machine shop (623 E. Adams St.; 602-258-8300, pizzeriabianco.com). A couple of other restaurants fill out the remaining buildings.

5 McFarland State Historic Park

24 Ruggles St., Florence, AZ 85232; 520-868-5216
azstateparks.com/mcfarland

A small town full of history between Phoenix and Tucson, Florence has more than 100 historic homes. McFarland State Historic Park is located in the oldest standing courthouse in Arizona, built in 1878 and named after Ernest McFarland, author of the GI Bill and the only person to have served in all three branches of Arizona government: two at the state level, as governor and an Arizona Supreme Court justice, and one at the federal level, as a US senator. The park/museum has interesting exhibits on the history of the area, and the building itself is listed on the National Register of Historic Sites. The docent here is very helpful, with information on the region, so it's a great place to stop and gather information on local attractions. Each February, the annual **Historic Florence Home Tour** showcases local homes and other historical structures.

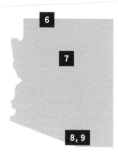

6 Pipe Spring National Monument

406 N. Pipe Spring Road, Fredonia, AZ 86022; 928-643-7105
nps.gov/pisp

One aspect of Arizona history that we don't hear much about is the Mormon settlers who came through here. As is common in the desert, the presence of a spring signifies a good gathering place, and the Kaibab Paiutes settled here, with Europeans and then Mormons arriving in the 19th century. Surrounded by the Kaibab Reservation, Pipe Spring National Monument recreates the conditions the Mormons faced when they traveled along the Honeymoon Trail through Utah and Arizona. Tours are conducted daily, although the hours are reduced during the winter. This monument is way off the beaten path, but if you're in the vicinity of the North Rim en route to Utah, it's worth a stop.

7 Riordan Mansion State Historic Park

409 W. Riordan Road, Flagstaff, AZ 86001; 928-779-4395
azstateparks.com/riordan-mansion

The Riordan brothers were lumber barons who played a critical role in establishing the town of Flagstaff. In the late 1800s, they came to Flagstaff to run the Arizona Lumber & Timber Company. When two of the Riordan brothers married two Metz sisters, they built adjacent log homes, connected in the center by a family room. Built in 1904, the Riordan Mansion is the world's largest Arts and Crafts–style duplex. The architect was Charles Whittlesey, a student of Louis Sullivan who designed the Grand Canyon's El Tovar Hotel (see page 59). You can stroll through the grounds at no charge, but to see the interior with its many original furnishings, you must join a guided tour ($12 adults, $6 kids 7–13).

8 Tubac Presidio State Historic Park

1 Burruel St., Tubac, AZ 85646; 520-398-2252
azstateparks.com/tubac

Most people, myself included, associate Tubac with an eclectic artisan community, but the history here goes much further back than that: the Tubac Presidio is estimated to be the oldest European settlement in Arizona. So many cultures, from Indian to Spanish to Mexican and European, have had impacts on the history of Arizona, and Tubac Presidio State Historic Park is a great place to see how each of these cultures contributed to the state's development. There's a wonderful Day of the Dead celebration and other fun events throughout the year. Combined with a visit to **Tumacácori National Historical Park** (see below) and the village of Tubac, this makes a perfect day trip from Tucson.

9 Tumacácori National Historical Park

1891 I-19 Frontage Road, Tumacácori, AZ 85640; 520-377-5060
nps.gov/tuma

Located 45 minutes south of Tucson, Tumacácori National Historical Park now sits where Jesuit missionary Father Eusebio Francisco Kino set up the mission church San José de Tumacácori in 1691. Before that, a branch of the O'odham people lived here along the Santa Cruz River. Visitors can join a guided tour or explore the mission and museum at their own pace. The **Juan Bautista de Anza National Historic Trail** passes through here, and you can take this trail for 4 miles to reach the **Tubac Presidio State Historic Site** (see above). The park hosts a number of special events; my favorite is the luminaria display on Christmas Eve, with thousands of paper lanterns scattered throughout the mission and surrounding grounds.

Historic Sites

Arizona Museum of Natural History, Mesa, AZ

I AM ADMITTEDLY AN OUTDOORSY TYPE, and the
climate and topography are what brought me to Arizona, but
I've been blown away by the diversity and quality of museums
here. No matter what part of the state you find yourself in, you're
bound to find museums dedicated to Arizona history and the Wild
West along with nature, science, and art. You just never know
what kind of museum you're going to stumble on when traveling
through Arizona.

ARIZONA HISTORY:
History Museums

Arizona Capitol Museum, Phoenix, AZ

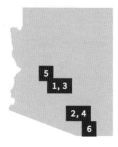

1 Arizona Capitol Museum

1700 W. Washington Ave., Phoenix, AZ 85007; 602-926-3620
azlibrary.gov/azcm

Arizona's capital bounced around many times before settling in Phoenix in 1889, which is when construction began on the Capitol building. While the state government and governor's office eventually moved to more-modern offices, the Capitol earned a spot on the National Register of Historic Places and became a museum in 1977. If you're interested in history, this is a great first stop when you arrive in Arizona so that you can understand the background of the territory and how Arizona became a state, as well as learn about such momentous events in Arizona history as Martin Luther King's visit in 1964 and the sinking of the USS *Arizona* at Pearl Harbor in 1941.

2 Arizona History Museum

949 E. Second St., Tucson, AZ 85719; 520-628-5774
arizonahistoricalsociety.org

This Tucson museum is located just across the street from the University of Arizona campus. Run by the Arizona Historical Society (which also oversees Flagstaff's Pioneer Museum and the Arizona Heritage Center in Tempe, among others), this museum depicts the history of Tucson and Southern Arizona from Spanish Colonial through modern times. More than a dozen individual rooms tell the story of a different era: from John Slaughter and the Slaughter Ranch to the Arizona Mining Hall, and a room about Geronimo and how his name evolved into legend. There is also a very moving display room dedicated to the events surrounding the January 2011 shootings at an event for US Representative Gabby Giffords in Tucson. The museum will validate your parking in the nearby garage.

3 Arizona Museum of Natural History

53 N. Macdonald, Mesa, AZ 85201; 480-644-2230
arizonamuseumofnaturalhistory.org

With one of the largest collections of dinosaur skeletons in the West, the Arizona Museum of Natural History in downtown Mesa is fun for kids of any age. While the museum has a distinct Arizona focus, the exhibits touch on all of the Southwest region. Started by amateur archaeologists, the museum has grown to become the largest dinosaur repository in Arizona. Starting in the **Origins Gallery,** visitors take a walk through time before reaching **Dino Mountain,** a very cool animatronic exhibit showing layers of time. Hourly "flash floods" are a must-see. The **Hohokam Room** showcases some of the history of Arizona's original residents, as well as an impressive basket collection from all cultures of North America. The building itself is historic, and you can still see the basement jail cells from 1884. In the historic courtyard, kids can pan for gold in a stream or dig for bones in the dinosaur pit. Closed on Mondays and holidays.

4 Arizona State Museum

1013 E. University Blvd., Tucson, AZ 85721; 520-621-6302
statemuseum.arizona.edu

Located on the University of Arizona campus, the Arizona State Museum is the oldest and largest anthropology museum in the Southwest. The museum also contains the largest collection of American Indian basketry, with more than 35,000 pieces. There's a nice mix of permanent and rotating collections. When I visited, two changing exhibits were focused on pottery and the evolution of Hopi Katsina dolls. Permanent collections include a basketry display that also allows you a glimpse into the large basketry vault. The **Paths of Life** hallway walks visitors through 10 Native groups from Northern Mexico to Northern Arizona, showing traditions from the past to the present.

5 Desert Caballeros Western Museum

21 N. Frontier St., Wickenburg, AZ 85390; 928-684-2272
westernmuseum.org

Located in the Wild West town of Wickenburg, the Desert Caballeros Western Museum is dedicated to preserving the art, history, and culture of the American West. In a town known as the "Dude Ranch Capital of Arizona," it seems they know a bit about Western culture here. Explore the history of the West through fine art, rotating exhibits, and an impressive calendar of events. The annual **Cowgirl Up** event each spring features contemporary female artists working in the Western genre.

6 Fort Huachuca Historical Museum

41401 Grierson Ave., Fort Huachuca, AZ 85613; 520-533-3638
history.army.mil/museums/tradoc/forthuachuca

From the late 1800s through World War II, as many as 20,000 Buffalo Soldiers were based here. Because the museum is located on an active

military base, visitors without military ID will need to show identification and fill out some paperwork. Once you're on the base, though, admission to the museum is free. In addition to the Buffalo Soldier exhibit, the museum provides a great overview of the history of the fort, which is particularly interesting if you have friends or family members who served here. There's also a **Military Intelligence Museum** on the grounds, also with no admission charge. The museum is closed Sundays, Mondays, and federal holidays.

History Museums

7 Hall of Flame Fire Museum

6101 E. Van Buren St., Phoenix, AZ 85008; 602-275-3473
hallofflame.org

One of the world's largest firefighting museums, the Hall of Flame in Phoenix is dedicated to the history of firefighting and the memory of firefighters lost in the line of duty. Over 10,000 objects make up the collection, including some dating back to the 18th century. There are more than 100 wheeled pieces in the collection, including a fire truck for kids to climb on. Learn how firefighting has evolved from horse-drawn wagons to modern fire engines. The **National Firefighting Hall of Heroes** is a moving tribute to more than 2,000 firefighters who have died in the line of duty since 1981. The museum is interactive and educational, as kids (and adults) can learn all about fire safety.

8 International Wildlife Museum

4800 W. Gates Pass Blvd., Tucson, AZ 85745; 520-629-0100
thewildlifemuseum.org

A nonprofit extension of the Safari Club International Foundation, the International Wildlife Museum sits in a castlelike building just off Gates Pass outside of Tucson. (The building is modeled after a French Foreign Legion outpost in Chad, Africa, that the founder visited while on safari.) The mission of this natural-history museum is conservation and appreciation of the world's wildlife; it is also an homage to the art of taxidermy, with dozens of dioramas featuring over 400 species of mammals, birds, and insects, including prehistoric animals. An entire room is dedicated to Teddy Roosevelt's conservation legacy, and **McElroy Hall** is essentially a huge trophy room featuring the spoils of the Safari Club's founder, C. J. McElroy. A small gift shop sells snacks, beverages, and gifts.

9 Mohave Museum of History and Arts

400 W. Beale St., Kingman, AZ 86401; 928-753-3195
mohavemuseum.org

For an overview of Northwest Arizona history, Mohave Museum is the place. For a very small fee, visitors also get access to the **Arizona Route 66 Museum** and the historic **Bonelli House.** Western film fans will appreciate the special Andy Devine exhibit celebrating this hometown Hollywood success (I learned about him for the first time here). The museum presents a varied assortment of exhibits with respect to Arizona history, from the various Native groups to trains and mines to a collection of presidential portraits.

10 Museum of Northern Arizona

3101 N. Fort Valley Road, Flagstaff, AZ 86001; 928-774-5213
musnaz.org

"Celebrating the Colorado Plateau since 1928" in a beautiful stone building at the edge of a pine forest, the Museum of Northern Arizona is a great attraction in Flagstaff. Using the map you receive upon entry, you follow the flow of the museum through **Geology & Paleontology** and then **Archaeology** into the **Native Peoples** exhibit. The orientation wall is the best example I've seen of the chronological evolution of Native Americans, from Paleo-Indian to contemporary Hopi and Navajo tribes, along with a traditional Hopi kiva display. The **Babbitt Room** features jewelry and ceramics from the Pueblo, Hopi, Navajo, and Zuni. Four rooms feature rotating art exhibitions, while the **Discovery Room** has games, crafts, and books for kids. Check the website for heritage festivals and special events, such as Navajo weaving talks and Hopi flute performances.

11 Phoenix Police Museum

180 W. Jefferson St., Phoenix, AZ 85003; 602-534-7278
phxpdmuseum.org

Housed in historic City Hall, this museum highlights the evolution and accomplishments of the Phoenix Police Department since its inception in 1881. The museum includes a Memorial Room dedicated to fallen officers, along with exhibits on the *Miranda vs. Arizona* decision and women on the police force, among others. They also have various police vehicles on display, including a helicopter. This small museum is worth a stop for anyone interested in law enforcement.

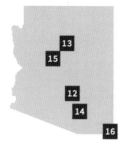

12 Pinal County Historical Museum

715 S. Main St., Florence, AZ 85132; 520-868-4382
pinalcountyhistoricalmuseum.org

This eclectic collection of historical items focuses on the Southwest and Pinal County. From prehistoric Indian exhibits to artifacts from the nearby Arizona State Prison, the museum has something for every interest. Exhibits include a ranch and cowboy display, a collection of Tom Mix memorabilia, cactus furniture, and a reference library with more than 1,000 books and a collection of *Arizona Highways* magazines dating back to 1937.

13 Pioneer Museum

2340 N. Fort Valley Road, Flagstaff, AZ 86001; 928-774-6272
arizonahistoricalsociety.org/museum/pioneer-museum

The Arizona Historical Society manages the Pioneer Museum, in a 1908 building that originally served as the Coconino County Hospital for the Indigent. The Pioneer Museum has hundreds of historic artifacts and photos depicting the lives of early Northern Arizona pioneers. Upstairs, former hospital rooms have been converted to "decade rooms" that depict local life from the 1890s to the 1960s; major local and US events are chronicled alongside interesting tidbits about the lifestyles of each decade, including the cost of living. Downstairs, you'll find rotating exhibits and a gift shop. The museum continues outside, with artifacts displayed around the museum grounds: a 1929 locomotive, a 1940s caboose, a 1915 Ford Model T, and a refurbished 1908 log cabin.

14 Presidio San Agustín del Tucson Museum

196 N. Court Ave., Tucson, AZ 85701; 520-837-8119
tucsonpresidio.com

See how Tucson got its start at a re-creation of the original Tucson Presidio. While not much is left of the original fort, it's easy to see how Tucson looked in the late 18th century. Included in the museum are a Native pit house discovered here, as well as historic Sonoran Row homes. After cruising the museum, head out on the **Turquoise**

Trail. This historic self-guided walking tour of downtown Tucson takes visitors on a tour of the Presidio District as well as downtown Tucson; a brochure narrates each stop along the painted turquoise stripe painted on the sidewalks. Check the calendar for special events, including living-history days.

15 Sharlot Hall Museum

415 W. Gurley St., Prescott, AZ 86301; 928-445-3122
sharlothallmuseum.org

Sharlot Hall was a pioneer woman both literally and figuratively, her family having settled near Prescott in the late 19th century. She loved storytelling and the written arts, and in 1909 she was appointed Arizona Territorial Historian, making her the first woman to hold a salaried position in the territory. Over a lifetime of travel and public office, Hall amassed an impressive collection of artifacts and documents, which now reside in the Old Governor's Mansion in Prescott. The Heritage campus surrounding the Old Governor's Mansion is a living-history museum with seven buildings covering 3.5 acres right in town. Guided tours can be prearranged, or you can meander through at your own pace, chatting with docents in the various buildings. Historical exhibits date back to the Clovis, a prehistoric Paleo-Indian culture. The second Saturday of each month brings history to life with themed programs led by staff in period dress.

16 Slaughter Ranch Museum

6153 Geronimo Trail, Douglas, AZ 85607; 520-678-7596
slaughterranch.com

"Texas John" Slaughter was an early settler of Southeast Arizona. This legendary figure was a Civil War veteran, cattle driver, rancher, and eventually the sheriff of Cochise County. The Slaughter Ranch, outside Douglas, played host to many historic events and migrations throughout the years. The Apache Wars unfolded on and around the property, with Sheriff Slaughter present for the capture of Geronimo. Pancho Villa was no stranger to the ranch during the Mexican Revolution. These days, the ranch is on the National Register of Historic Places and is open to the public Wednesday–Sunday. Part of the road to the ranch is unpaved, so call ahead to check road conditions if there have been recent rains. The John Slaughter exhibit at the **Arizona History Museum** in Tucson (see page 48) augments this visit nicely.

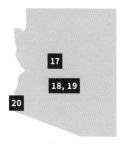

17 The Smoki Museum

147 N. Arizona Ave., Prescott, AZ 86301; 928-445-1230
smokimuseum.org

The Smoki People (pronounced "smoke-eye") were a fraternal organization formed in the 1920s as a way to raise funds for Prescott's Frontier Days Rodeo. In a gross example of cultural appropriation, the fictitious tribe staged "Indian shows" where they dressed up as Native Americans and performed for the crowds. (Senator Barry Goldwater was an "antelope dancer" in the group, which lasted into the 1980s.) Ironically, these mock performances were wildly popular even though American Indians nationwide weren't allowed to practice their own religions until 1978; eventually, however, the group had trouble recruiting new members. What remains of their collections is now the Smoki Museum, housed in a Civilian Conservation Corps building from 1935. Today, the museum's mission is "to instill understanding and respect for the indigenous cultures of the Southwest," and its board now partners with Native advisors to present this unique history.

18 Wells Fargo History Museum

145 W. Adams St., Phoenix, AZ 85003; 602-378-1852
wellsfargohistory.com/museums/phoenix

Wells Fargo has free history museums all over the country, including this one in downtown Phoenix. Wells Fargo opened in 1852 and played a key role in the expansion into the Western states with banking and mail delivery to the Pacific Coast. The museums allow you to experience America's exciting gold rush heyday and the role that Well Fargo played in the colorful history of the Wild West. Through the stagecoach experience, you can learn what it was like to travel 5 miles per hour across the plains in a stagecoach. The many artifacts on display include an original 1860 Concord stagecoach, solid-gold nuggets, and a working telegram machine that you can use to send messages the old-fashioned way. An art gallery also features the Douglas Collection of Western Art.

19 Western Spirit: Scottsdale's Museum of the West

3830 N. Marshall Way, Scottsdale, AZ 85251; 480-686-9539
scottsdalemuseumwest.org

Just steps from Old Town Scottsdale, the Western Spirit Museum celebrates the art, history, and stories of the American West, encompassing 19 states plus part of Mexico and Canada. The building alone is worth the price of admission: designed by a local architect and LEED Gold certified, the exterior is designed to represent basket weaving and saguaro ribs. Inside, the variety of exhibits is astounding, from the world's greatest collection of Western movie posters to Old West and Contemporary West art galleries and an original pipe tomahawk used by Meriwether Lewis in the early 1800s. You can easily spend hours exploring the two-story museum and sculpture garden. Fortunately, your admission includes same-day reentry.

20 Yuma Territorial Prison Museum

220 N. Prison Hill Road, Yuma, AZ 85364; 928-783-4771
yumaprison.org

Set on a bluff overlooking what's left of the Colorado River before it empties into the Gulf of California, the Yuma Territorial Prison opened in 1876. Thirty-six years before Arizona became a state, it's rumored that the territorial Legislature was handing out assignments and Yuma, vying for capital city, got the prison instead. This "desert Alcatraz" was known as the toughest prison of the Old West, but it operated for only 33 years until the state prison was moved to Florence, where it remains today. At the current site, visitors get a brochure for a self-guided tour, much of which is outdoors. The guard tower and view deck offer nice views out over the river, while the cell block and "dark cell" give you an idea of prisoner conditions in the late 19th century. A small on-site museum shows an informative movie about the prison's history.

Bright Angel Trail, Grand Canyon National Park

ARIZONA IS THE GRAND CANYON STATE, so even though this natural wonder of the world encompasses a National Park, outdoor adventures, stargazing, Native American history, and Arizona history, I feel it deserves a chapter all its own. In 2019 Grand Canyon National Park celebrated its 100-year anniversary and became an official Dark Sky Park. Although the park receives more than six million visitors per year, only 1% of them drop below the rim to explore beyond the viewpoints. Here are just a few ways you can experience the Grand Canyon during your visit.

RECREATION & THE OUTDOORS:
The Grand Canyon

1 1, 4, 2, 3
5

1 Grand Canyon Village

Grand Canyon South Rim, Grand Canyon Village, AZ 86023; 928-638-7888
nps.gov/grca

Most Grand Canyon visitors come to the South Rim as it's where the bulk of visitor services are located. It's possible to visit on a day trip from Flagstaff, Tusayan, or Williams, but there are plenty of activitie to occupy a few days as well. Free shuttles travel most of the South Rim, so once you arrive and find a parking spot, you can walk and use the shuttles to explore the sites here. Grand Canyon Village includes all of the lodging for the South Rim as well as the **Bright Angel Trailhead,** the start of one of the main routes into the canyor Make sure to stop at the **National Geographic Visitor Center** for the IMAX movie. There are many dining and shopping options, with more available at the nearby **Market Plaza.** Every viewpoint is differ ent, so be sure to allow time to explore them all and soak in the vas expanse of the Grand Canyon.

2 Grand Canyon North Rim

AZ 67, North Rim, AZ 86052; 877-386-4383
grandcanyonforever.com

Only 10% of Grand Canyon visitors come to the North Rim, and access is a big reason for that. While the North Rim facilities are onl 10 miles across the canyon from the South Rim, the drive is actually 220 miles. There are also far fewer services at the North Rim, but that is part of the reward for making the drive. Several accessible trails go to various viewpoints along the rim and the side canyons. There is one lodge with rooms, cabins, a couple of dining options, a campground, a gas station/general store, and a visitor center. It's important to note that the North Rim (8,000' elevation) is closed in the winter, typically mid-October–mid-May; extreme winter conditions are common during this period, so the road is closed.

3 Desert View Watchtower

Grand Canyon Village, AZ 86023; 928-638-7888
nps.gov/grca/planyourvisit/desert-view.htm

If you're coming in from the east, Desert View is the perfect place to start your visit to Grand Canyon National Park and your first opportunity for a grand glimpse of the canyon. Located along the South Rim at the east end of the park, this seven-story stone tower was designed by architect Mary Colter in 1932. A quick climb of the tower offers breathtaking views for 100 miles, as well as a nice look at some of the rapids on the Colorado River. Inside, there are several murals from Hopi artist Fred Kabotie, as well as a gift shop and visitor center. A few short trails lead to lookout spots over the river. *Note:* Desert View is not serviced by the Grand Canyon shuttles, so you'll need to drive here.

4 El Tovar Hotel

Grand Canyon Village, AZ 86023; 888-297-2757
grandcanyonlodges.com/lodging/el-tovar-hotel

Many National Parks have a grand lodge, and the Grand Canyon is no exception. El Tovar opened as a Harvey House hotel in 1905, the same year the Grand Canyon received national-monument (now national-park) status. Built of rustic stone and pine, the 78-room lodge sits at the edge of the South Rim, offering astounding canyon views from guest rooms and the dining room. Rooms start just above $200 per night, and reservations open up 13 months in advance, so a multiday stay requires some serious advance planning during high season. Alternatively, you can enjoy a gourmet meal in the dining room. For non–hotel guests, reservations are accepted 30 days in advance.

5 Grand Canyon Caverns

AZ 66, Peach Springs, AZ 86434; 928-422-3223
gccaverns.com

Discovered in 1927, this is one of the largest dry caves in the world and soon became a popular tourist spot along Historic Route 66. Located near the Hualapai Reservation, this is best combined with a visit to the **Skywalk** (see page 61) and **West Rim** facilities or en route to **Havasu Falls.** The campground here is a popular spot for those continuing on or returning from Havasu Falls. These days, the caverns are an all-in-one adventure stop, with five cave tours ranging from a 25-minute short tour to a 2.5-hour Wild Tour. For the truly adventurous, there's a "cave motel"—a motel room 200 feet below ground.

6 Various locations

6 Grand Canyon Helicopter Tours

Various operators; see below or check online for more options

Another exciting way to see the Grand Canyon is from the seat of a helicopter, and there are several operators offering tours of the canyon. Although some of the canyon's airspace is restricted for environmental reasons, there's enough scenery for everyone. Most day trips are fairly short rides that leave from Tusayan. The Hualapai tribe at **Grand Canyon West** offers helicopter tours that land at the bottom of the canyon and include a short rafting tour (call 888-868-9378 or see grandcanyonwest.com/explore/west-rim/helicopter-aerial-tours for details); establishments such as **Bar 10 Ranch** (435-628-4010, bar10.com) offer helicopter rides in and out of the canyon as well. Be prepared to pay a premium, but know that you'll never have better views of the canyon than those you can get from a helicopter! (*Tip:* Wear black so that your clothes aren't reflected in your photos.)

7 Grand Canyon Mule Rides

South Rim; 303-297-2757
grandcanyonlodges.com/plan/mule-rides

The Grand Canyon mules are an iconic part of the park, and a great way to explore below the rim for those who aren't interested in hiking the trails. Mules were the original transportation method of the Grand Canyon, so it's only fitting to see how the pioneers explored the canyon. Day-trippers can take a Canyon Vista ride along the South Rim; for a truly special experience, you can ride the mules down the Bright Angel Trail to **Phantom Ranch** for an overnight stay at the bottom of the canyon.

8 Grand Canyon Railway

Grand Canyon Village, AZ 86023; 800-843-8724
thetrain.com

Arrive at the Grand Canyon in style on the Grand Canyon Railway. With daily departures from Williams and a second departure in peak season, passengers can relax and bypass all traffic to the South Rim.

The journey takes about 2 hours to reach the Grand Canyon Depot, just steps from the edge of the canyon. The schedule allows for approximately 4 hours to explore the South Rim and Grand Canyon Village before departing back to the Williams Depot. Passengers choose from six classes of service, from Pullman Class to the Luxury Dome car. "Stay and save" packages combine the train ride with an overnight stay at the Grand Canyon Railway Hotel in Williams.

9 Grand Canyon Skywalk

808 Eagle Point Road, Peach Springs, AZ 86434; 928-769-2636
grandcanyonwest.com

Owned by the Hualapai tribe, the Skywalk is part of the larger Grand Canyon West complex, which offers a whole host of visitor activities. The main attraction, though, is the Grand Canyon Skywalk, a glass-bottom walkway extending 70 feet over the canyon where you can look between your feet to the canyon floor 4,000 feet below you. The rules are quite strict, however, and you cannot bring anything with you on the walkway—not even a phone or camera—so any photographic proof you want from your visit will have to be purchased from the gift shop. (A lot of people complain about this part, but if you know ahead of time, it's still a really cool experience.) You can also arrange other tours at Grand Canyon West, including helicopter rides, rafting trips, and a zip-line experience.

Watson Lake, Prescott, AZ

IN ARIZONA'S DESERT ENVIRONMENT, water is rare and celebrated. Surprisingly, there are six lakes within a 75-minute drive of Phoenix, and other lakes and waterfalls are scattered throughout the state. Arizona also lays claim to the two largest man-made lakes in the United States. Stumbling upon a lake, or even a puddle, can sometimes be quite a surprise. Here are a few of the best lakes and waterfalls that you can reach on an Arizona day trip. (Unfortunately, the iconic **Havasu Falls,** is not a day-trip destination, as it involves a 20-mile round-trip hike.)

RECREATION & THE OUTDOORS:
Lakes & Waterfalls

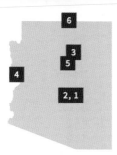

1 Apache Lake Marina & Resort

Roosevelt, AZ 85545; 928-467-2511
apachelake.com

There are four major lakes along the Salt River above Phoenix; Apache Lake lies between Roosevelt Lake and Canyon Lake. The last 7 miles of the road from Phoenix are unpaved and a bit of a washboard, but that helps keep the crowds down compared to Canyon Lake and Saguaro Lake. At 17 miles long, it's the second largest of the four lakes after Roosevelt Lake. The full-service Apache Lake Marina rents pontoon boats, while the resort has three motels, a restaurant, a saloon, and a campground. US Forest Service campgrounds are also scattered around the lake.

2 Canyon Lake

16802 AZ 88, Apache Junction, AZ 85119; 480-288-9233
canyonlakemarina.com

The third of four reservoirs above Phoenix, Canyon Lake has 28 miles of shoreline to explore. The full-service Canyon Lake Marina has boat rentals, supplies, a restaurant, and a campground with 28 RV sites and 18 tent sites. A highlight of Canyon Lake is the *Dolly Steamboat*, which has been plying the waters of Canyon Lake since the 1980s. They offer several daily cruises, including a Twilight Dinner Cruise and an Astronomy Cruise. If you're short on time, the Scenic Nature Cruise is just 90 minutes long.

3 Grand Falls

Little Colorado River, Leupp, AZ

Few people know that Arizona has a waterfall that is taller than Niagara Falls. The catch: it's seasonal. The falls are formed on the Little Colorado River as it makes it way towards the confluence of the Colorado River in the Grand Canyon. The falls are on Navajo land, about an hour northeast of Flagstaff. Although they're located on a dirt road, it's passable in a passenger car, but if it has rained recently (which is when the falls are running), you can run into some ruts. Nevertheless, the site of these "chocolate" falls (a reference to their brownish water) is pretty spectacular, especially in the middle of the desert.

4 Lake Havasu

Lake Havasu City, AZ
lhcaz.gov

Lake Havasu was formed by Parker Dam, the world's deepest dam, in 1938. In the 1960s, real estate developers started bringing potential buyers out from the Midwest, and Lake Havasu soon became Arizona's playground. With more than 300 days of sunshine, Lake Havasu attracts over 800,000 visitors per year. The lake has 27 replica lighthouses placed around the shore, along with several boat-in campgrounds tucked into scenic coves. If you don't have your own boat, head to the quaint **English Village** along the channel in Lake Havasu City, where tour operators are waiting to take you out on the water. *Note:* This is a popular college spring-break destination, so choose your dates accordingly.

5 Lake Mary

12 miles southeast of Flagstaff on AZ 3; 928-527-3600

In the Flagstaff region, Lake Mary is the destination for water recreation. The Lake Mary Recreation Corridor includes Upper and Lower Lake Mary. Upper Lake Mary is popular with boaters, as there is no motor size limit. Lower Lake Mary can be seasonal, tending to dry up during drought years, although it's great for fishing, when it has water. **Lake Mary Country Store** (8510 Lake Mary Road; 928-774-1742, lakemarycountrystore.com) rents fishing boats, canoes, kayaks, and paddleboards.

6 Lake Powell

Page, AZ

While the creation of Lake Powell was quite controversial (see Glen Canyon Dam, page 35) and no doubt covered up some spectacular desert scenery, it's one of the most beautiful lakes I've ever seen, and second only to Lake Mead as the largest artificial reservoir in the United States. My first glimpse of Lake Powell came at the end of a rafting trip through Canyonlands when we took a Cessna flight from Hite Marina at the north end of the lake. My second trip to Lake Powell was on a camping trip to Page where I enjoyed several days of spectacular sunsets over the lake. Overnight houseboat trips are one of the most popular ways to experience Lake Powell, but there are many day-trip options as well, including boat rentals and kayaking tours. In September I was able to find a beach near the Wahweap Marina that was completely deserted, which is quite a treat given the popularity of Page.

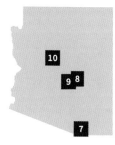

7 Patagonia Lake State Park

400 Patagonia Lake Road, Nogales, AZ 85621; 520-287-6965
azstateparks.com/patagonia-lake

Southern Arizona is decidedly lacking in lakes and waterfalls, save a trickle or puddle during monsoon season. That makes Patagonia Lake State Park a popular destination for Southern Arizona residents. Covering 265 acres, this man-made lake is a prime location for wildlife spotting, fishing, boating, hiking, and camping. A special birding trail leads 0.5 mile to **Sonoita Creek,** which draws lots of birds; look for blue herons, hummingbirds, and kingfishers along the creek's riparian zone. At an elevation of just over 4,000 feet, this area has temperatures that are often about 10° cooler than those in Tucson, so if you're visiting in summer, you might want to make this more than a day trip!

8 Roosevelt Lake

28085 AZ 188 N., Roosevelt, AZ 85545; 602-977-7170
rlmaz.com

Arizona's largest lake is the first of the four lakes along the Salt River above Phoenix. Created in 1911 with the construction of a dam, it's also Arizona's oldest man-made reservoir. There are two ways to reach Roosevelt Lake: along the Apache Trail, past Apache Lake, or coming down south on AZ 188 from Payson. Part of the Apache Trail was closed in 2019 due to wildfire, so be sure to check road conditions before heading out. Once you reach Roosevelt Lake, there are tons of services and activities to enjoy. You can rent pontoons, ski boats, Jet-Skis, and all kinds of water toys to go with your boat rental. A convenience store, campground, and lodging options are also nearby. Don't miss a visit to the cliff dwellings at **Tonto National Monument** (see page 76), which overlooks Roosevelt Lake.

9 Saguaro Lake

14011 N. Bush Highway, Mesa, AZ 85215
saguarolakemarina.com

Of the four reservoirs on the Salt River above Phoenix, Saguaro Lake is the closest one to the Phoenix metro area. Just over 20 miles of shoreline offer endless recreational opportunities. Start your visit at the marina, which has boat rentals, fishing supplies, and fuel. If you prefer to let someone else drive the boat, the **Desert Belle** has been touring Saguaro Lake for more than 50 years. A 90-minute narrated cruise runs daily, while live music and wine cruises are offered weekly. Campgrounds are located at **Saguaro del Norte Recreation Area** and **Bagley Flat,** which is accessible only by boat.

10 Watson Lake

3101 Watson Lake Park Road, Prescott, AZ 86301; 928-777-1122
prescott.com/watson-lake

Absolutely one of the coolest lakes in Arizona, Watson Lake (along with nearby **Willow Lake**) originates in the Granite Dells of Prescott, giving it an eerie backdrop of boulders and hoodoolike features. While you can get some nice views of the lake from various parking lots in the park, the best way to see it is from a kayak (rentals on-site) or by hiking the 5-mile trail around the lake. A disc-golf course at the lake occasionally intersects with the hiking trail. (**Lynx Lake** and **Goldwater Lake** are two other Prescott lakes with nice hiking trails.) At an elevation of more than 5,000 feet, Watson Lake and its cooler temperatures provide a welcome reprieve from the Valley heat.

Lakes &
Waterfalls

Canyon de Chelly National Monument, Chinle, AZ

ARIZONA HAS A TOTAL of 24 National Park Service units—more than any other state in the US. This includes three National Parks, plus many National Monuments and recreation areas. It's safe to say that a **National Parks Pass** is a worthy investment for anyone spending time in Arizona (see nps.gov/planyourvisit/passes.htm for details). Just look at all the sites you'll have access to!

RECREATION & THE OUTDOORS:
National Park Sites

Signal Hill petroglyphs, Saguaro National Park, Tucson, AZ

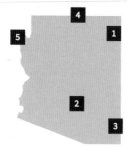

1 Canyon de Chelly National Monument

About 2.8 miles east of US 191 off Indian Route 7, Chinle, AZ 86503; 928-674-5500
nps.gov/cach

Canyon de Chelly (pronounced "Shay") took my breath away the first time I visited, and it quickly became one of my favorite spots in Arizona. Located on the Navajo Reservation, the canyon is administered by the National Park Service. Navajo people still live and farm here, so travel within the canyon is allowed only when you're accompanied by a park ranger or Navajo guide. The one exception is the **White House Ruins Trail,** a 3-mile round-trip hike that's open to all visitors. Anasazi and Ancestral Puebloan ruins dot the canyon, and a guided tour will give you insight into the native history of the canyon. The two rim drives (**North Rim,** 35 miles round-trip; **South Rim,** 37 miles round-trip) offer amazing views into the canyon. The iconic and sacred **Spider Rock** is an 800-foot sandstone spire along the South Rim drive. Lodging and tourist services are available in the park at **Thunderbird Lodge** or in nearby Chinle.

2 Casa Grande Ruins National Monument

1100 W. Ruins Drive, Coolidge, AZ 85128; 520-723-3172
nps.gov/cagr

A perfect spot to stretch your legs on the drive between Phoenix and Tucson, the Casa Grande ruins are an impressive structure. The **Great House,** estimated to be more than 600 years old, stands four stories tall. It's one of the few ruins I've visited that is now under a shelter, which was built in 1903. Thankfully, this site has been in the hands of the National Park Service since 1918. Casa Grande is credited to the Hohokam, who also pioneered irrigation techniques that are seen throughout the Phoenix area. The Casa Grande site also contains a small museum and visitor center.

3 Chiricahua National Monument

12856 E. Rhyolite Creek Road, Willcox, AZ 85643; 520-824-3560
nps.gov/chir

An eerie landscape unlike anything else I've seen in Arizona, Chiricahua National Monument sits in the southeast corner of the state. At an elevation just over 5,000 feet, it's often much cooler than the desert and a good shoulder season hiking destination. The monument has both outdoor activities and historic information, making it an excellent day trip destination. Start your trip at the Visitor Center to plan out your day and grab a map. Take the scenic drive to **Massai Point,** where you can access a network of hiking trails. If the timing is right, join a guided tour of **Faraway Ranch,** home to Swedish settlers who owned this property from 1887 until 1975 and operated a guest ranch for many of those years.

4 Glen Canyon National Recreation Area

Page, AZ 86040; 928-608-6200
nps.gov/glca

Glen Canyon National Recreation Area includes more than 1 million acres along the Colorado River from the Utah border to Lee's Ferry near the Grand Canyon. It includes **Lake Powell** (see Lakes & Waterfalls chapter, page 65); **Glen Canyon Dam** (see Historic Buildings & Architecture chapter, page 35); **Horseshoe Bend** (see Odds & Ends chapter, page 142); and **Rainbow Bridge National Monument.** With nearly 2,000 miles of shoreline, the recreational opportunities are endless. Some areas, such as Rainbow Bridge, are still important Navajo sites, so check in at the visitor center to see where you can and cannot go.

5 Lake Mead National Recreation Area

601 Nevada Way, Boulder City, NV 89005; 702-293-8990
nps.gov/lake

Lake Mead was created when Hoover Dam (see page 35) was erected and is one of the largest reservoirs in the United States. This was also America's first national recreation area, and being less than 1 hour from Las Vegas, it's an extremely popular destination for boaters, hikers, and sightseers. The recreation area includes Lake Mohave and extends all the way down to Laughlin. The main visitor center is near Boulder City and Hoover Dam, while the three marinas are the usual entry point onto Lake Mead. Houseboating is hugely popular, but you can rent anything from a kayak to a houseboat. **Lake Mead Cruises** (866-292-9191, lakemeadcruises.com) also offers paddlewheel tours.

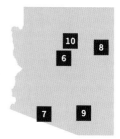

6 | Montezuma Castle National Monument

Camp Verde, AZ 86322; 928-567-3322
nps.gov/moca

Just off I-17 in the Verde Valley, Montezuma Castle National Monument is an impressive cliff dwelling that sits in a recessed cliff face 100 feet above the valley floor. The building originally contained about 20 rooms spread across five stories. Like other ruins in the area, this is a southern Sinagua site from around the 12th century and was abandoned by the 14th century. A 0.3-mile interpretive trail takes visitors past the cliff dwellings. **Montezuma Castle,** though incorrectly named after the Aztec emperor, was one of the first National Monuments in the United States. In addition to the cliff dwellings, the monument includes nearby **Montezuma Well,** a limestone sinkhole used for irrigation.

7 | Organ Pipe Cactus National Monument

10 Organ Pipe Drive, Ajo, AZ 85321; 520-387-6849
nps.gov/orpi

You can see organ pipe cactus at botanical gardens around Arizona, but if you want to see the only place where they grow wild in the United States, you'll have to visit Organ Pipe Cactus National Monument. This UNESCO Biosphere Reserve protects more than 300,000 acres of wild land along the Mexico border. The park has a complicated history with migration, and Border Patrol presence is heavy along the park roads. Start your visit at the **Kris Eggle Visitor Center,** where rangers are available to make recommendations. The **Desert View Trail,** a 1-mile loop from the campground, gives a nice overview of the cactus, with scenic views of the surrounding mountains. The park also has two scenic drives: **Ajo Mountain Drive** is a 21-mile loop, and **Puerto Blanco Drive** is a 41-mile loop.

8 | Petrified Forest National Park

1 Park Road, Petrified Forest, near Holbrook, AZ 86028; 928-524-6228
nps.gov/pefo

One of Arizona's lesser known parks, Petrified Forest National Park is a great stop on a road trip along I-40, as the highway cuts right through the park. The Painted Desert unit on the north side of I-40 offers breathtaking badlands views at several points along the road. If you can catch this at sunset, it's stunning. The **Painted Desert Inn,** a National Historic Landmark, houses a museum of history and architecture. As you follow the park road, you'll cross over I-40 and enter the Petrified Forest area. Along the way, you'll see petroglyphs and ancestral Puebloan homes, as well as several areas with a high concentration of petrified wood. There are short hikes and trails along the way, all of which are dog-friendly. If you want some petrified wood to take home as a souvenir, don't snatch it out of the park—you'll find plenty for sale (or free) in the nearby town of **Holbrook.**

9 Saguaro National Park

3693 S. Old Spanish Trail, Tucson, AZ 85730; 520-733-5153
nps.gov/sagu

This unique National Park, comprising two units separated by the city of Tucson in the middle, protects nearly 100,000 acres of saguaro cactus habitat. The Rincon Mountain District on the east side of Tucson and the Tucson Mountain District on the west side of Tucson each offer stunning scenery. Each district offers a visitor center, scenic drive and hiking trails. The highlight of the Rincon Mountain District is the **Cactus Forest Loop,** an 8-mile paved road with dramatic views of the Catalina Mountains. In the Tucson Mountain District, petroglyphs are easily accessible at **Signal Hill,** and the **Bajada Loop Drive** is a 5-mile trip on a gravel road. Arriving in the Tucson Mountains via **Gates Pass** is worth the trip.

10 Sunset Crater Volcano National Monument

6082 Sunset Crater Road, Flagstaff, AZ 86004; 928-526-0502
nps.gov/sucr

Formed sometime between AD 1040 and 1100, Sunset Crater resulted from the most recent eruption in this volcano-rich region. Any high point in the region will offer views of several smaller cinder cones, evidence of the volcanic activity here. In fact, the volcanic texture, and unique topography made this an ideal training site for several Apollo astronauts prior to their missions to the moon. At Sunset Crater Volcano National Monument, there are several overlook trails along the main road, as well as a 1-mile loop at the **Lava Flow Trail.** In conjunction with **Wupatki National Monument** (page 77), Sunset Crater Volcano National Monument is a great side trip on your drive from Flagstaff to the Grand Canyon. The entire loop road is 35 miles, so allow a couple of hours to see the highlights.

11 Tonto National Monument

26260 AZ 188 N., Roosevelt, AZ 85545; 928-467-2241
nps.gov/tont

A rare example of the Salado culture from the 14th century, Tonto National Monument preserves two cliff dwellings high above Lake Roosevelt, 100 miles east of Phoenix. The lower cliff dwelling is reached by a steep, 1-mile round-trip trail. Eleven rooms are mapped out at the lower cliff dwellings; grab a guide from the ranger stationed at the dwelling. If you wish to visit the **Upper Cliff Dwelling**, you must join a guided tour. Tours are offered Friday–Monday in November–April; advance reservations are required, as space is limited. Also note that the **Lower Cliff Dwelling Trail** is open only from 8 a.m. until noon during the summer.

12 Tuzigoot National Monument

25 Tuzigoot Road, Clarkdale, AZ; 928-634-5564
nps.gov/tuzi

In the heart of the Verde River Valley, this Southern Sinagua pueblo once supported up to 8,000 residents at its peak, around AD 1300. Named after the Apache word for "crooked water," Tuzigoot ruins sit on a small hill overlooking the river and surrounding valley. At one time, there were two stories with 87 ground-floor rooms in the main pueblo. Visitors can circle around the exterior on a short, paved path and visit the indoor museum exhibits. For a different view of Tuzigoot, take a drive over to **Dead Horse Ranch State Park** in Cottonwood (675 Dead Horse Ranch Road; 928-634-5283, azstateparks.com/dead-horse). Admission to Tuzigoot includes admission to **Montezuma Castle National Monument** (see page 74).

13 Vermilion Cliffs National Monument

Just north of US 89A, Page, AZ; 435-688-3200
blm.gov/visit/vermilion-cliffs

This National Monument near Page, covering nearly 300,000 acres of land along the Utah–Arizona border, encompasses **Paria Canyon, Coyote Buttes,** and the **Vermilion Cliffs.** Paria Canyon is typically seen on an overnight backpacking trip, and Coyote Buttes is home to

The Wave. These sandstone formations are photo-famous but notoriously hard to get into: only 20 permits are sold each day through a lottery system. If, like me, and you're unable to get into The Wave, check out the **White Pocket** area of Paria Canyon; on a short hike, you can catch astounding views and landscapes. Although this is a National Monument, it's managed by the Bureau of Land Management and doesn't have the visitor facilities you might expect from the National Park Service.

4 Walnut Canyon National Monument

3 Walnut Canyon Road, Flagstaff, AZ 86004; 928-526-3367
nps.gov/waca

Not far from Flagstaff, Walnut Canyon National Monument preserves cliff dwellings of the Sinagua people, who lived here more than 800 years ago. At one time, as many as 400 people lived at this settlement, before abandoning the cliff dwellings just 100 years after they were built. Eventually, the Sinagua people assimilated into Hopi culture, and Walnut Canyon remained untouched until the late 19th century, when the railroad started to bring tourism to this region. After a few years of pillaging by souvenir hunters, Walnut Canyon became a National Monument in 1915. Start in the visitor center to watch a brief movie and get an understanding of the site; then hike the 1-mile round-trip **Island Trail** for a better view of the cliff dwellings. There are several viewpoints along the way, and you descend first, so make sure you have the energy to climb back out at the end of the hike! For a flatter hike, the **Rim Trail** is only 0.7 mile and has interpretive signage along the rim of the canyon.

15 Wupatki National Monument

25137 N. Sunset Crater–Wupatki Loop Road, Flagstaff, AZ 86004; 928-679-2365
nps.gov/wupa

Another ancient pueblo near Flagstaff is the Wupatki Pueblo, which was built and occupied in the 1100s AD by Ancestral Puebloan people. The location is at the crossroads of many cultures; Sinagua, Cohonina, and Kayenta Anasazi all passed through here, and their traditions are seen in various aspects of the remaining pueblos. More than 100 different types of pottery have been discovered at Wupatki. Much like Walnut Canyon, these pueblos were only occupied for 100 years or so, before the inhabitants moved on. Today, there are three main areas to visit in the National Monument, all of which are a short stroll from the parking areas. Wukoki Pueblo is down a side road as you approach from Sunset Crater. Wupatki Pueblo, the largest, is located behind the Visitor Center. As you approach US 89 on the north end of the loop road, there are several pueblos: **Lomaki Pueblo, Citadel Pueblo, Nalakihu Pueblo,** and the **Box Canyon Dwellings.**

Catalina State Park, Tucson, AZ

APPROXIMATELY 72% OF LAND in Arizona is public—more than 35 million acres—which means there's a lot of space to get outside and have an adventure! Arizona also has more mountain peaks (3,928) than any of the other mountain states. Of course, outdoor adventure is woven through many activities in this book, especially in the National Parks and Grand Canyon chapters. Outdoor adventure can be had in nearly every corner of the state, so these are just a few quintessential experiences to seek out.

RECREATION & THE OUTDOORS:
Outdoor Adventures

Antelope Canyon X, Page, AZ

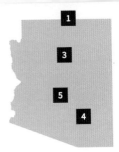

2 Various locations

1 Antelope Canyon

22 S. Lake Powell Blvd., Page, AZ 86040; 855-574-9102
antelopecanyon.com

The most expensive photograph ever sold is a photo of Antelope Canyon, which sold for $6.5 million in 2014. Today, a visit to Antelope Canyon is on everyone's Arizona bucket list. All of the local slot canyons are on Navajo land, so you must have a guide to enter them. Tours of the Upper and Lower Canyons are available; Upper Antelope Canyon is the photo-famous destination where light and dust combine for fantastic photography each afternoon. If you don't want to be shuttled through with herds of other tourists for a quick snapshot, you can pay extra for a photographer's tour, which is the only way you can bring a tripod along. As the popularity of this area grows, similar canyons nearby are opening for tours. Just down the road, I enjoyed a tour of Antelope Canyon X for half the price, with fewer people and much more time to explore the canyon on my own.

2 Arizona National Scenic Trail

From the Mexico–Arizona border to the Arizona–Utah border
aztrail.org

It doesn't get more adventurous than hiking 800 miles from Mexico to Utah through the state of Arizona. The Arizona National Scenic Trail was created in the 1980s and became a National Scenic Trail in 2009, joining 10 other trails that include the Pacific Crest Trail and the Appalachian Trail. The trail is divided into 43 sections, many of which are popular with backpackers and day hikers. Starting at the Coronado National Memorial along the Mexican border, the trail passes through the Santa Catalina Mountains, the Superstition Mountains, and, of course, the Grand Canyon.

Outdoor Adventures

3 Arizona Snowbowl Ski Resort

9300 N. Snowbowl Road, Flagstaff, AZ 86001; 928-779-1951
snowbowl.ski

Snow skiing in Arizona? You betcha! Just outside of Flagstaff is the Arizona Snowbowl on the western slope of Mount Humphreys. Lifts rise to 11,500 feet and offer views all the way to the Grand Canyon. There are 55 ski runs served by eight lifts, and the slopes are generally open from mid-November through the end of April. Three terrain parks are available for all skill levels, and even ski bikes are allowed. In all other seasons, the lift is open for hikers and mountain bikers, or those who just wish to enjoy the scenery. Grab a picnic basket at the **Agassiz Lodge Sport Shop,** and plan to spend a day on the trails. In the fall, Snowbowl and the road leading to it are great places to see fall color on the aspen trees. Nearby, **Arizona Nordic Village** (16848 US 180; 928-220-0550, arizonanordicvillage.com) offers cross-country skiing and snowshoe trails.

4 Arizona Zipline Adventures

35406 S. Mount Lemmon Road, Oracle, AZ 85623; 520-308-9350
ziparizona.com

Just north of Tucson in the town of Oracle, you'll find Arizona Zipline Adventures, Arizona's first zip-line ecotour. Set on the back side of Mount Lemmon, the scenery here is pretty stunning, with panoramic views of the Galiuro Mountains. The Eco Tour package includes five zip lines, which slowly increase in height and speed until you work your way up to the grand finale, a 1,500-foot line that brings you back to where the tour started. It's exhilarating and the hardest part is taking that first step off the platform. After your tour, be sure to have lunch at the **Peppersauce Kitchen** before going on your way.

5 Camelback Mountain

4925 E. McDonald Drive, Phoenix, AZ 85018
climbcamelback.com

Camelback Mountain is one of the prominent peaks within Phoenix city limits and one of the most popular hikes for locals and visitors. The short but steep hike offers sweeping views of the surrounding valley, but it's not for the faint of heart. Two trails lead to the summit at 2,680 feet. The address provided here is for the **Echo Canyon Trailhead,** the start of a 1.25-mile trail to the summit. The **Cholla Trail** is a more technical trail with steep drop-offs and loose gravel, so it's less popular than the Echo Canyon trail. Although each hike is less than 5 miles round-trip, hikers are rescued from Camelback frequently due to the harsh conditions of the desert. I always carry twice as much water as I think I'll need.

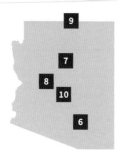

6 | Catalina State Park

11570 N. Oracle Road, Tucson, AZ 85737; 520-628-5798
azstateparks.com/catalina

One of my favorite spots for hiking in the Tucson area, Catalina State Park is a beautiful spot for birders, hikers, and horseback riders. If you're visiting during summer monsoons or winter rains, call ahead to make sure the trails and park are open, as the entrance road sometimes floods and many trails cross a large wash. One of my favorite hikes is the 2.3-mile **Canyon Loop Trail,** which has minimal elevation gain and astounding views. The trail to **Romero Pools** is a strenuous but rewarding workout that is 2.8 miles each way. The trail continues all the way to **Mount Lemmon** if you're so inclined. There is also a 1-mile **Birding Trail** loop for a short hike. The park also has 120 campsites equipped with electricity and water (flush toilets and showers available).

7 | Flagstaff Extreme Adventure Course

2446 Fort Tuthill Loop, Flagstaff, AZ 86001; 888-259-0125
flagstaffextreme.com

Located in Flagstaff's Fort Tuthill County Park, this adventure course takes zip-lining up a notch. The site has an adult adventure course and one for kids, each with a set of increasingly difficult challenges that will test your physical determination. (At an elevation of nearly 7,000 feet, no less!) Make your way through zip lines, obstacles, rope swings, climbing walls, and more, with bailout options at every point. If a traditional zip line is more your speed, there are more than 30 to sample at the adventure course. One of the best things about this course is that it's in a public park, so others can tag along and watch from below and take photos of the participants.

8 Granite Mountain Hotshots Memorial State Park

AZ 89 (about 50 miles southwest of Prescott), Yarnell, AZ 85362; 877-697-2757
azstateparks.com/hotshots

On June 30, 2013, 19 members of the Granite Mountain Hotshots firefighting team died while battling the Yarnell Hill Fire. The devastating events of that day made this one of the deadliest wildfires in US history, and it was later portrayed in the 2017 movie *Only the Brave*. Arizona's first Memorial State Park opened in November 2016 to honor the 19 men and their families from nearby communities. The park comprises the 7-mile round-trip **Hotshots Trail**, which has 19 granite plaques scattered along the way, one for each firefighter. The trail ends at the Observation Deck, where hikers can look out over the Fatality Site below. The hike is strenuous, but you can reach the first plaque, honoring Superintendent Eric March, with just a 0.25-mile hike.

9 Kayak Lake Powell

816 Coppermine Road, Page, AZ 86040; 928-660-0778
kayakpowell.com

The beauty of Lake Powell is best seen from the water, where you can get into secret coves and find deserted beaches. Most visitors travel Lake Powell by houseboat or motorboat, but to really experience the natural beauty, you can't beat a kayak tour of the lake. With a personal watercraft, you can get into nooks and crannies that bigger boats can't reach. If you aren't familiar with the lake or don't have strong navigation skills, I highly recommend going out with a tour guide. Not only will they get you back safely, they'll have a few hidden spots up their sleeves to share with you. There are also tours that combine a hike to Antelope Canyon with your day on the water.

10 McDowell Sonoran Preserve

18333 N. Thompson Peak Parkway, Scottsdale, AZ 85255; 480-312-7013
mcdowellsonoran.org

More than 30,000 protected acres in Scottsdale offer opportunities for hiking, biking, rock climbing, and horseback riding on 215 miles of trails. The preserve is one of the largest urban sanctuaries in the US, and more than 600 volunteers donate their time to lead educational programs and guided hikes. Trail options range from the 0.5-mile **Bajada Loop** to the 11-mile **Tom's Thumb/East End Loop.** Guided hikes are offered from mid-October through April, and private guided hikes can be arranged. Start your visit at the **Desert Discovery Center.**

11 Picacho Peak State Park

15520 Picacho Peak Road, Eloy, AZ 85131; 520-466-3183
azstateparks.com/picacho

This funny-looking peak sits right off I-10 between Phoenix and Tucson. One of the best times to visit the park is during spring wild-flower season, as there are fields of poppies and lupines. The park has several hiking trails, a campground, and day-use areas. Climbing the 3,400-foot peak is a popular endeavor for many hikers. Much like Camelback Mountain (see page 83), the distance of this trail (2.7 miles round-trip) can be deceiving. It's incredibly steep—so much so that cables and railings have been installed on the upper portion to help hikers pull themselves up to the summit. Between wildlife and wildflowers, it's a great park to explore, whether you summit Picacho Peak or not.

12 Sedona Jeep Tour

Pink Adventure Tours, 204 AZ 89A N., Sedona, AZ 86336; 800-873-3662
pinkadventuretours.com/tours/sedona-tours

Pink Adventure Tours have been showing tourists around Sedona for over 50 years and have expanded to other popular areas like Las Vegas and the Grand Canyon. When I originally went out with Pink in 2008, there were just two options for jeep tours: scenic or technical. Now, they have tons of different tours, but I would still recommend the **Mogollon Rim** scenic tour, or if you want to see what jeeps are made for, take the **Broken Arrow** tour. Other options include visits to Sinagua ruins and day trips to the Grand Canyon or Antelope Canyon. I prefer to leave the driving to the professionals, but for those with the skills and the right vehicle, there are tons of 4WD trails around Sedona.

13 Salt River Rafting

Arizona Outback Adventures, 17645 N. 93rd St., Scottsdale, AZ 85255; 866-455-1601
aoa-adventures.com

The Lower Salt River flows out of Saguaro Lake's Stewart Mountain Dam and is a popular place for float trips and rafting. Weekends bring hundreds of partying tubers and boaters, so a midweek trip is highly recommended. Arizona Outback Adventures has half-day rafting and kayak tours. Departing from their Scottsdale office, a 40-minute drive transports you to Tonto National Forest. Punctuated by a few riffles and small rapids, it's a leisurely float that takes you through gorgeous desert scenery. If you're lucky, you'll spot the resident wild horses who live here, as well as several birds and other animals. There are plenty of opportunities for swimming along the way. Life jackets, snacks, water, and a group dry bag are provided. Bring sunscreen, a hat and shoes, and clothing that you don't mind getting wet.

14 Sabino Canyon

5700 N. Sabino Canyon Road, Tucson, AZ 85750; 520-749-8700
fs.usda.gov/recarea/coronado/recarea/?recid=75425

One of the premier hiking destinations in Tucson, Sabino Canyon is one of my favorite spots in Southern Arizona. The great news is that it's not just for hikers: a tram system carries visitors 3.5 miles into the canyon, with nine stops along the way. With a purchased ticket, you can hop on or hop off the tram at any stop, or you can just go along for the ride. There is usually water flowing, and there are a few beaches along the road where you can hang out and cool off. Dozens of well-marked hiking trails crisscross the canyon, from easy interpretive strolls to difficult trails that climb the canyon walls. One of my favorite hikes is the **Seven Falls Trail** in adjacent Bear Canyon. Because Sabino Canyon is part of the National Park System, your National Parks Pass is good here; otherwise, it's $5 to park for the day. Bring cash in case you need to park in the overflow lot, which does not have an attendant.

15 Slide Rock State Park

6871 AZ 89A, Sedona, AZ 86336; 928-282-3034
azstateparks.com/slide-rock

Tucked along Oak Creek in Oak Creek Canyon just outside Sedona, Slide Rock State Park is a natural waterslide and swimming hole. Under the shade of sycamores and cottonwoods, swimmers flock from all over to experience the 80-foot slide. Smaller slides and wading pools offer alternate options for all ages. If you visit in the fall, you may get the added bonus of apple picking at the **Pendley Homestead,** an apple orchard that predates the park. If you visit in the summer, plan to arrive very early, or expect to wait in line to enter. On my last visit, on a Monday in June, each car had to wait until another car left before being admitted to the parking lot.

Chicago Cubs spring training at Sloan Park, Mesa, AZ

EVERY SPRING, thousands of baseball fans flock to Arizona for spring-training practice and exhibition games. Sixteen Major League Baseball teams play in Arizona's Cactus League, spread across 10 stadiums in metro Phoenix. Pitchers and catchers report for spring training in early February, with the rest of the team joining in mid-February. Exhibition games last through the end of March, when all teams return home in advance of opening day. Baseball fans love spring training, with affordable tickets, intimate atmosphere, and warm weather.

RECREATION & THE OUTDOORS:
Sports

CACTUS LEAGUE BASEBALL
cactusleague.com

Arizona Diamondbacks, Salt River Fields
7555 N. Pima Road, Scottsdale, AZ 85258; 480-270-5000
saltriverfields.com

Chicago Cubs, Sloan Park
2330 W. Rio Salado Parkway, Mesa, AZ 85201; 480-668-0500
mlb.com/cubs/sloan-park

Chicago White Sox, Camelback Ranch
10710 W. Camelback Road, Phoenix, AZ 85037; 623-302-5000
mlb.com/camelback-ranch

Cincinnati Reds, Goodyear Ballpark
1933 S. Ballpark Way, Goodyear, AZ 85338; 623-882-3130
goodyearbp.com

Cleveland Indians, Goodyear Ballpark
1933 S. Ballpark Way, Goodyear, AZ 85338; 623-882-3130
goodyearbp.com

Colorado Rockies, Salt River Fields
7555 N. Pima Road, Scottsdale, AZ 85258; 480-270-5000
saltriverfields.com

Kansas City Royals, Surprise Recreation Campus
15960 N. Bullard Ave., Surprise, AZ 85374; 623-222-2222
surpriseaz.gov/2679/recreation-campus

Los Angeles Angels, Tempe Diablo Stadium
2200 W. Alameda Drive, Tempe, AZ 85282; 480-350-5265
tempe.gov/government/community-services/community-recreation-centers
/diablo-stadium

Los Angeles Dodgers, Camelback Ranch

10710 W. Camelback Road, Phoenix, AZ 85037; 623-302-5000
mlb.com/camelback-ranch

Milwaukee Brewers, Maryvale Baseball Park

3600 N. 51st Ave., Phoenix, AZ 85031; 623-245-5500
mlb.com/brewers/spring-training/ballpark

Oakland Athletics, Hohokam Stadium

1235 N. Center St., Mesa, AZ 85201; 480-644-4451
mesaparks.com/parks-facilities/hohokam-stadium

San Diego Padres, Peoria Sports Complex

16101 N. 83rd Ave., Peoria, AZ 85382; 623-773-8700
peoriasportscomplex.com

San Francisco Giants, Scottsdale Stadium

7408 E. Osborn Road, Scottsdale, AZ 85251; 480-312-2586
scottsdaleaz.gov/scottsdale-stadium

Seattle Mariners, Peoria Sports Complex

16101 N. 83rd Ave., Peoria, AZ 85382; 623-773-8700
peoriasportscomplex.com

Texas Rangers, Surprise Recreation Campus

15960 N. Bullard Ave., Surprise, AZ 85374; 623-222-2222
surpriseaz.gov/2679/recreation-campus

Verde Canyon Railroad, Clarkdale, AZ

TRAINS AND PLANES are an integral part of Arizona's history. The arrival of rail lines hastened the development of Arizona communities as pioneers and cowboys rushed to the West. Trains ushered in the era of tourism at the Grand Canyon, and many Arizona towns owe their existence to the railways, whether from tourism or mining. The wide-open spaces of the desert make for excellent military presence as well, and the US Air Force makes up the bulk of the military population in Arizona. Both airplanes are railroads are well represented in Arizona attractions and museums.

ON THE GO:
Airplanes & Railroads

1 Arizona Railway Museum, *Chandler* *94*
Tour several refurbished train cars, including a 1927 Pullman car at this outdoor
attraction near Phoenix.

2 Commemorative Air Force Airbase Arizona, *Mesa* *94*
Learn about the Commemorative Air Force, tour several hangars of vintage
planes, or go for a ride in a warbird.

3 Kingman Railroad Museum, *Kingman* *95*
Learn how Kingman was founded, and wave to the *Southwest Chief* as it makes
the daily pass en route to Los Angeles from Chicago.

4 Pima Air & Space Museum, *Tucson* *95*
This premier air museum has more than 300 aircraft, including a Boeing 787
Dreamliner and a former Air Force One aircraft.

5 Pinal Airpark, *Marana.* *95*
See where 747s go to retire or get spruced up and flipped for new owners.

6 Planes of Fame Air Museum, *Williams* *96*
Explore dozens of historic aircraft, including several from WWII, at this museum
near the Grand Canyon.

7 Southern Arizona Transportation Museum, *Tucson* *96*
Visit Tucson's Amtrak station for a historical tour of how the railroad shaped the
history of Tucson.

8 Titan Missile Museum, *Green Valley* *96*
Tour this site and learn all about the US missile program during the Cold War.

9 Verde Canyon Railroad, *Clarkdale* *97*
Climb aboard this scenic train ride that takes you from the lush Verde Valley to
the red-rock country near Sedona.

3

1, 2

5
4

1 Arizona Railway Museum

330 E. Ryan Road, Chandler, AZ 85286; 480-821-1108
azrymuseum.org

The Arizona Railway Museum is a must for any train enthusiast. The railroad plays a strong role in Arizona's history; between mining and tourism, train travel has been a critical link to the outside world. At any given time, there are several refurbished cars open to tour at your own leisure. The 1927 Pullman superintendent's car is a fascinating glimpse into the opulence of the past. Another car shows various seat configurations from dozens of train lines, from Canadian National to a Dallas Streetcar. Visitors will spend most of the time out in the train yard walking through gravel, so wear good walking shoes. Inside the small museum, you'll find smaller mementos of travel, including tableware and ashtrays from some of the train lines. Hours are limited to weekends Labor Day–Memorial Day (closed in summer).

2 Commemorative Air Force Airbase Arizona

2017 N. Greenfield Road, Mesa, AZ 85215; 480-924-1940
azcaf.org

Located at Falcon Field in Mesa, the air base is operated by the Commemorative Air Force, an international organization dedicated to preserving combat aviation history. The Arizona Airbase is the largest of 80 units around the world, with hundreds of exhibits housed in the 55,000-square-foot museum and hangars. Visitors can walk around freely to get an up-close look at several airplanes, including the only airworthy example of a Lockheed Vega DL-1. If admiring these birds from afar isn't enough for you, the Airbase offers warbird rides. Prices range from $80 for a cabin seat in a Beechcraft C-45 Expeditor to $850 for a nose seat in a Boeing B-17G Bomber. Open-cockpit tours are also offered seasonally.

3 Kingman Railroad Museum

402 E. Andy Devine Ave., Kingman, AZ 86401; 928-718-1440
thekingmanrailroadmuseum.org

The Kingman Railroad Museum is a working Amtrak station; the adobe
building went up in 1907 and is listed on the National Register of Historic
Places. Amtrak's *Southwest Chief* makes a daily stop here on its route
from Chicago to Los Angeles. The museum is small but has several
displays on the history of the railroad, and how it shaped the town of
Kingman. In fact, the name *Kingman* was taken from a railroad surveyor.
Three working model train tracks are worth a few minutes of entertainment, plus there's memorabilia from the golden age of train travel.

4 Pima Air & Space Museum

6000 E. Valencia Road, Tucson, AZ 85706; 520-574-0462
pimaair.org

Airplane fans must visit the Pima Air & Space Museum when visiting
Tucson. This is one of the world's largest aerospace museums, and its
proximity to Davis-Monthan Air Force Base means you're likely to see
some planes in action during your visit. The museum includes over 350
aircraft on display in the six hangars and outdoor areas. See a Blue
Angels jet and an Air Force One from JFK's presidency. For a small
additional fee, you can join a narrated tram tour of the museum
grounds. I highly recommend adding on the Boneyard tour, but you
must make reservations at least 10 business days in advance. A background check is required due to the sensitivity of the area, so you'll
need to provide a Social Security number (or passport number if you're
not a US citizen) when making your reservation.

5 Pinal Airpark

24641 E. Pinal Airpark Road, Marana, AZ 85653; 520-682-4181
pinalcountyairpark.com

As you travel up I-10 from Tucson to Phoenix, you might notice dozens
of Boeing 747s lined up off to the west. This is Pinal Airpark, a public
airport and storage facility with a rich history; it was built in 1942, just
after Pearl Harbor. Over 10,000 pilots were trained here, including up
to 1,000 Chinese pilots recruited to fight against Japan. In 1948 the
government transferred the site to Pinal County for use as a public
airport. The runway averages one operation per day, so the real draw
is the airplanes here for maintenance, storage, reactivations, or
destruction. When I visited, there were around 100 airplanes, down
from a peak of 250 right after 9/11. You can get up close and personal
with several 747s, including a TWA relic. Complimentary tours are
conducted by appointment only; contact jim.petty@pinalcountyaz.gov
to schedule a tour.

6 Planes of Fame Air Museum

755 S. Mustang Blvd., Williams, AZ 86046; 928-635-1000
planesoffame.org

A great stop for aviation fanatics en route to the Grand Canyon. The museum includes one of the most extensive collections of historic aircraft, with over 160 planes on display between this location and the sister location in Chino, California. The collection includes several WWII aircraft and a replica 1903 Kitty Hawk Flyer. As a living museum, Planes of Fame has an extensive flight schedule that lets visitors see these planes in action. Many aircraft are lent out to traveling exhibitions, so the collection changes often. The museum is closed October 31–March 31.

7 Southern Arizona Transportation Museum

414 N. Toole Ave., Tucson, AZ 85701; 520-623-2223
tucsonhistoricdepot.org

Before the arrival of rail service to Tucson in 1880, the town was a remote outpost in the Wild West. This connection to the rest of the country put Tucson on the map and gave residents access to new goods that were not previously available. The highlight of this small museum at the Tucson train station is Locomotive No. 1673, which was featured in the 1955 musical *Oklahoma!* During operating hours, visitors can tour the locomotive and even sit in the driver's seat. Inside, there are two rooms of mementos, mostly from the Southern Pacific Railroad, which was the first to serve up train service to Tucson.

8 Titan Missile Museum

1580 W. Duval Mine Road, Green Valley, AZ 85614; 520-625-7736
titanmissilemuseum.org

The Titan Missile Museum is a National Historic Landmark about 45 minutes south of Tucson. This well-preserved missile site is a fascinating glimpse into Cold War history. The Titan Missile site played a critical role in the peaceful conclusion of the Cold War; a recurring theme you'll hear throughout the museum is "peace through deterrence," which suggests that the mere threat of a nuclear missile—also known as MAD, or mutually assured destruction—was enough to ensure peace with Russia. There were a total of 54 Titan II missiles in the US, and some were also used to launch satellites and space shuttles. Guided tours take you into the bowels of missile command and simulate an actual missile launch. Allow time before or after your tour for exploring the exhibit gallery.

9 Verde Canyon Railroad

300 N. Broadway, Clarkdale, AZ 86324; 800-582-7245
verdecanyonrr.com

This scenic train ride takes you through the Verde Valley of Northern Arizona. There are daily departures for this 4-hour ride, which travels 20 miles along the Verde River, from Clarkdale to Perkinsville and back again. Passengers can choose from first-class cars or coach, but everyone has access to open-air cars, which is where you'll get the best views. Travel in style in Pullman and Budd Chair cars from the 1940s, and take in the history of the canyon, starting with Sinagua cliff dwellings along the rails just after Clarkdale. Check the website for special departures, such as Rails and Ales, or Summer Saturday Starlight tours.

US 60, Salt River Canyon, Globe, AZ

THE WIDE-OPEN DESERT is made for road trips. As I criss-crossed the state several times to research this book, I was continually stunned by the changing landscapes of Arizona and the beautiful drives along the way. No matter which corner of the state you're in, you can find a scenic drive nearby.

ON THE GO:
Scenic & Iconic Drives

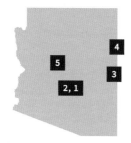

1 Apache Trail

AZ 88 from Apache Junction to Roosevelt Dam

Often cited as the most scenic drive in Arizona, the Apache Trail was originally a stagecoach trail through the Superstition Mountains. The trail starts just east of Mesa at Apache Junction and continues for 40 miles to Roosevelt Dam. The first interesting stop is **Goldfield Ghost Town** (see page 27), followed by **Lost Dutchman State Park, Tortilla Flat** (see page 29), and then the three Salt River lakes: **Canyon, Apache,** and **Roosevelt.** The last half of the road is unpaved but navigable for passenger cars. Alternatively, jeep tours are available if you'd rather leave the driving to someone else. Most travelers make a loop of the drive by coming back through **Globe** on US 60. This loop allows you to visit **Tonto National Monument** (see page 76) and **Boyce Thompson Arboretum** (see page 112) on the way back.

2 Beeline Highway

AZ 87 from Fountain Hills to Payson

Another scenic day trip from Phoenix, the Beeline Highway follows AZ 87 from the foothills northeast of Phoenix up to the Mogollon Rim at Payson. The road quickly climbs out of the desert up to pine forests and cooler temperatures at 5,000 feet elevation. In addition to gorgeous scenery, interesting stops include **Saguaro Lake** and **McDowell Mountain Park.** For a full day, round-trip excursion, continue on AZ 87 past Payson through the small mountain towns of Strawberry and Pine, stopping at **Tonto Natural Bridge State Park** before cutting through Camp Verde to I-17. These roads are all paved, so there are no concerns with taking your rental car along for the drive.

3 Coronado Trail National Scenic Byway

US 191 from Springerville to Clifton

Was this the route Coronado took in search of the Seven Cities of Gold? Perhaps! Skirting the New Mexico border through Apache National Forest, the Coronado Trail National Scenic Byway takes you from Clifton to Springerville on what has been called the nation's curviest federal highway. While the entire route is paved, it's not for the faint of heart. There are more than 400 curves, including some hairpin turns, and the road climbs to an elevation of over 9,000 feet. Continue north past Springerville and 191 will take you past **Canyon de Chelly** (see page 72) and all the way to **Monument Valley** (see page 20) Or head back west into the mountain resort towns of **Show Low** and **Pinetop.** This route is also part of the multiday **Nugget Trail,** which makes a loop through Globe and Safford. Fun fact: the highway used to be Route 666, which earned it the nickname "the Devil's Highway."

4 Historic Route 66

US 66 from Chicago to Los Angeles

Fewer images evoke the nostalgia of the classic American road trip than a highway sign for Route 66. The route has several nicknames, including "the Mother Road" and "America's Main Street." The entire route from Chicago to Los Angeles covers over 2,400 miles. Towns and businesses boomed along the route only to founder in the late 1950s and early 1960s, when the Interstate Highway System was built and I-40 bypassed several of the small towns. Fortunately, American nostalgia helps keep Route 66 alive in Arizona, even as it parallels I-40 across much of the state. From "Standing on the corner in Winslow, Arizona" to locations that inspired the Pixar movie series *Cars* to the ghost town of Oatman and its wild burros, you can definitely drive Route 66 through Arizona on a day trip, but there's also enough to occupy you for a week or two if you have the time.

5 Route 89A

AZ 89A from Prescott to Flagstaff

This Northern Arizona route hits some of the best highlights in the state. Linking two of my favorite towns in Arizona, the whole ride is only 91 miles, but I could stretch this one out to two weeks with all of the fun stops along the way. Starting in Prescott, make your climb up to the "ghost town" of **Jerome** (see page 27) before descending into the Verde Valley towns of **Clarkdale** and **Cottonwood.** Some great side trips here include the **Verde Canyon Railroad** (see page 97) and **Tuzigoot National Monument** (see page 76). Continuing along, you'll see a sharp transition as you leave the pine forest and hit the **Red Rock Scenic Byway** through Sedona. Linger in Sedona as long as you can, then pop in for a dip at **Slide Rock State Park** (see page 87) before the road climbs to pine forests again as it follows Oak Creek to Flagstaff.

6 Salt River Canyon

US 60 from Globe to Show Low

One of my favorite drives in Arizona is to follow US 60 through Salt River Canyon—I will go out of my way for this one! The first time I took this route, en route to Holbrook and Petrified Forest, I thought I'd made a wrong turn and ended up at the Grand Canyon; it's *that* breathtaking (minus the tour buses and crowds). More than half of the route is on the Apache Reservation, so there aren't many services along the way. There's a rest area at the bottom of the canyon where the road crosses the Salt River and, on the other side, a small outpost of whitewater-rafting outfitters if the water is high enough. There are many pullouts along the way where you can stop and take photos of this breathtaking canyon.

7 Sky Island Scenic Byway

Catalina Highway from Tucson to Summerhaven

Sky islands are a unique phenomenon in the Southwest, when a high-elevation mountain is surrounded by desert. The Sky Island Scenic Byway, which climbs Mount Lemmon from Tucson, is a great way to experience the range of ecosystems in a sky island. Starting in a saguaro forest and climbing to an elevation of 7,800 feet in the tiny town of Summerhaven, the 25-mile drive takes about an hour each way, more if you stop along the way. There are some great hikes along the way, including **Babad Do'ag.** Some of the best viewpoints are at **Windy Point** and **Geology Vista.** As you enter the pine forests, there are several campgrounds and a lake at Rose Canyon. The town of **Summerhaven** is a great place to grab lunch, rent bikes, or start a hike. The chairlifts at **Mount Lemmon Ski Valley** (520-576-1321, skithelemmon.com) are open year-round; if you have reservations for the Sky Center, they meet at the Ski Valley. For a self-guided tour, download the University of Arizona's **Mount Lemmon Science Tour** app (iOS and Android) before you leave town.

Broad-billed hummingbird, Tucson, Arizona

SPENDING A FEW DAYS IN ARIZONA is enough to turn anyone into a birder. Arizona welcomes thousands of bird-watchers each year and has 42 designated Important Bird Areas identified by the Audubon Society. What's more, it's home to the greatest diversity of hummingbird species in the United States, with up to 15 species in all along the Mexico border from Texas to Arizona.

Here are some of the state's best spots for birding—don't forget your binoculars!

SCIENCE & NATURE:
Birding

1 Cave Creek Canyon

Forest Service Road 42, Portal, AZ 85632; 520-558-2221
friendsofcavecreekcanyon.com

Not to be confused with Cave Creek north of Phoenix, Cave Creek Canyon is located near the town of Portal in the Chiricahua Mountains. The higher elevation makes this an ideal spot for year-round bird-watching, and the remote location means fewer crowds to scare off the birds. **Cave Creek Ranch** (520-558-2334, cavecreekranch. com) offers overnight lodging, or visitors can pay $5 to bird-watch on the premises. Proximity to Mexico means you can spot birds here that are quite rare elsewhere in the United States.

2 Imperial National Wildlife Refuge

12812 Wildlife Way, Yuma, AZ 85365; 928-783-3371
fws.gov/refuge/imperial

This stretch along the Colorado River protects 30 miles of shoreline and several species who live in the Riparian Zone. The 1938 Imperial Dam created a wetlands area along the river, which provide feeding and nesting grounds for migratory birds and other wildlife. The Yuma clapper rail is a bird unique to this region, with an endangered population of less than 1,000 birds remaining. Begin your visit at the visitor center, where you can pick up maps and intel on current events. The refuge is open to hunters, so be sure to ask about locations and take all necessary precautions. *Note:* This is not the same location as Imperial Sand Dunes Recreation Area, which is a popular dune buggy destination in California.

3 Kofa National Wildlife Refuge

Palm Canyon Road, Yuma, AZ 85365
fws.gov/refuge/kofa

About 90 minutes north of Yuma, Kofa National Wildlife Refuge includes nearly 700,000 acres, most of which is designated wilderness. Much of the refuge is wild, without roads or services, but Palm Canyon is a popular spot as it's the only place in Arizona where palm trees are native. The Palm Canyon Trail is home to several bird species, including thrashers, canyon towhees, and gnatcatchers; the refuge was originally designated to protect bighorn sheep, so if you're lucky, you may spot one of those as well. This area once held a large number of mines, so use extreme caution when exploring off-trail.

4 Madera Canyon

Green Valley, AZ 85622
friendsofmaderacanyon.org

The Santa Rita Mountains lie south of Tucson, with the peak of Mount Wrightson looming nearly 9,500 feet over the valley floor. The higher elevation of Madera Canyon makes this a good hiking destination in the shoulder season when it's too warm elsewhere. The climate also makes Madera Canyon one of the top birding destinations in the country. A common sight is the elegant trogon, a bird I've only seen previously in Central America. If you want a shot at spotting one of more than 250 species of birds, **Santa Rita Lodge** is a great place to start (520-625-8746, santaritalodge.com). Their bird-watching station is open to the public, with feeders and seating, and the gift shop has birding checklists as well as seasonal information. For the full dawn-to-dusk experience, you can rent a cabin or casita and spend the night at the lodge.

5 Ramsey Canyon Preserve

27 E. Ramsey Canyon Road, Hereford, AZ 85615; 520-378-2785
nature.org/en-us/get-involved/how-to-help/places-we-protect
/ramsey-canyon-preserve

The Huachuca Mountains near Sierra Vista hold another important birding destination of Southern Arizona. Managed by The Nature Conservancy, the preserve offers guided walks (March–November), where you'll have a good chance at spotting hummingbirds, woodpeckers, and elegant trogons, as well as other wildlife such as coatimundis and wild turkeys. It's estimated that there are as many as 170 bird species here in the peak season. **Ramsey Canyon Inn** (520-378-3010, ramsey canyoninn.com) is a B&B at the heart of the birding action for those who want to stay overnight and be the first bird-spotters on the trail in the morning.

6 San Bernardino National Wildlife Refuge

Douglas, AZ; 520-364-2104
fws.gov/refuge/san_bernardino

Adjacent to the Slaughter Ranch Museum (see page 53), this wildlife refuge harbors nearly 300 species of birds. Located at the headwaters of the Yaqui River of Mexico, the area encompasses wetlands that

protect native species such as the Yaqui Chub and the Chiricahua Leopard Frog. The visitor center can provide up-to-date information, including any active hunting areas, as the refuge does open for seasonal quail, dove, and rabbit hunting. In addition to the myriad birds you can spot here, it's a great place to see butterflies, lizards, snakes, and javelinas.

7 San Pedro Riparian National Conservation Area

Cochise County, AZ; 520-439-6400
blm.gov/visit/san-pedro

The San Pedro River Valley is a large reason why Sierra Vista is called the "Hummingbird Capital of the World." Nearly 400 species of birds pass through here each year during migration and nesting seasons, including many hummingbirds. This area represents the northernmost range of the Gray Hawk and other Central American birds, making this a great spot to catch those "life list" species. Another attraction of the conservation area is the Murray Springs Clovis Site, an important archaeological site from North America's earliest inhabitants, who arrived here more than 10,000 years ago.

8 Sipe White Mountain Wildlife Area

Springerville, AZ 85938; 928-367-4281
azwildlifetrails.com/northeastern-arizona-wildlife-trails/sipe-white-mountain
-wildlife-area

Moving north to the White Mountains, the Sipe White Mountain Wildlife Area is a great spot to see hummingbirds during the summer migration, in addition to raptors, osprey, and hawks at various times in the year. Hiking trails wind through the property, affording opportunities to see birds and other wildlife, including antelopes, turkeys, and coyotes. The visitor center has a nice display on local wildlife, with animal pelts and other exhibits. The site also includes areas of archaeological interest, and the on-site ponds are great places to find ducks. The last Saturday in July is usually when an annual Hummingbird Festival takes place, with volunteer opportunities and educational sessions for all ages.

9 Whitewater Draw Wildlife Area

4423 W. Bagby Road, McNeal, AZ 85617; 520-642-3763
azgfd.com/wildlife/viewing/wheretogo/whitewater

The Sulphur Springs Valley draws thousands of sandhill cranes each winter as they migrate from northern climates. Arriving in early fall and staying as late as March, these cranes are celebrated with the annual **Wings Over Willcox Birding & Nature Festival,** held each year on Martin Luther King Jr. weekend. The festival offers tours on a number of subjects, including photography, biology, and, of course, birding; see wingsoverwillcox.com for more information. The nearby **Willcox Playa** is another important site for sandhill cranes in this area. Even if you can't make the festival, there's a pretty good chance of seeing loads of sandhill cranes anytime between November and February.

Birding

Tucson Botanical Garden, Tucson, AZ

THE BIODIVERSITY OF ARIZONA is a big draw, and much to my surprise, there are distinct seasons in every region of Arizona. The Sonoran Desert seems to have something in bloom nearly year-round, and the spring of 2019 brought a so-called superbloom to much of Arizona. Whether you want to explore the flora and fauna of the Sonoran Desert, the Mogollon Rim, or the pine forests of Northern Arizona, there are numerous gardens and arboretums to explore.

SCIENCE & NATURE:

Gardens, Flowers & Arboretums

1 The Arboretum at Flagstaff, *Flagstaff* *112*
Explore over 700 species of plants in the arboretum, surrounded by a pine forest
with hiking trails.

2 Arizona–Sonora Desert Museum, *Tucson* *112*
One of the best Tucson destinations, with hundreds of birds, plants, animals,
and special programs for all ages.

3 Boyce Thompson Arboretum, *Superior* *112*
Take a hike through 400 acres along Queen Creek in the Superstition Mountains.
Amazing scenery and educational opportunities.

4 Desert Botanical Garden, *Phoenix* *113*
A truly magical place to spend a day in Phoenix, this garden has more than
50,000 different plants and several themed walking loops.

5 Tohono Chul Botanical Gardens & Galleries, *Tucson* *113*
There's an impressive collection of Sonoran Desert plants in this botanical
garden, which is also a great place to spot wildlife right in town.

6 Tucson Botanical Gardens, *Tucson* *114*
In the heart of Tucson, 17 specialty gardens have themes representing various
regions of the world; there's a fun calendar of events to boot.

7 White Mountain Nature Center, *Lakeside* *114*
Get out of the desert for the cooler high country, and learn about the flora and
fauna of the White Mountains.

8 Yume Japanese Gardens, *Tucson* *114*
This peaceful escape from the bustle of Tucson has koi ponds, teahouses, and
a museum of Japanese art.

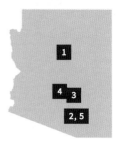

1 The Arboretum at Flagstaff

4001 S. Woody Mountain Road, Flagstaff, AZ 86005; 928-774-1442
thearb.org

Open May–October, The Arboretum at Flagstaff has over 700 species of plants that reflect the surrounding Coconino National Forest. Some of the highlights include a Southwest butterfly house, a mushroom garden (best visited during summer monsoons), and the Horticultural Center, where you can see volunteers hard at work. The 200-acre site includes about 2 miles of walking paths, all of which are dog-friendly. The **Outer Loop** trail takes you through the pine forest, with lovely views of the San Francisco Peaks and Lowell Observatory.

2 Arizona–Sonora Desert Museum

2021 N. Kinney Road, Tucson, AZ 85743; 520-883-2702
desertmuseum.org

Ranked by TripAdvisor as the number-one attraction in Tucson and one of the top 10 museums in the country, the Arizona–Sonora Desert Museum (ADSM) is one of my favorite places to spend the day. ASDM bills itself as a "fusion experience"—part zoo, part botanical garden, part aquarium, part natural-history museum, and part art gallery. Spread over nearly 100 acres adjacent to Saguaro National Park, 2 miles of trails wind through many desert habitats. Some of my favorite spots in the museum are the cactus garden, the hummingbird aviary, and the walk-in aviary. For children, the **Packrat Playhouse** is a fun interactive playground. The museum also has a fabulous gift shop, two restaurants, snack bars, and art galleries. Don't miss the **Raptor Free Flight** demonstration; hours vary by season.

3 Boyce Thompson Arboretum

37615 E. Arboretum Way, Superior, AZ 85713; 602-827-3000
btarboretum.org

Arizona's largest and oldest botanical garden feels more like a wilderness experience than a contained arboretum. At nearly 400 acres, the arboretum holds over 3,900 plants from around the world. Queen Creek flows through the grounds, set at the base of Picketpost Mountain, which makes a gorgeous backdrop for your visit. A 1.3-mile trail leads visitors through exhibits such as a cactus garden, aloe garden, herb garden, and palm and eucalyptus groves. Tours are conducted daily, January–May, and special events and classes are scheduled throughout the year. A small gift shop sells drinks and snacks.

4 Desert Botanical Garden

1201 N. Galvin Parkway, Phoenix, AZ 85008; 480-941-1225
dbg.org

A visit to the Desert Botanical Garden is a must when visiting Phoenix. Set in beautiful Papago Park, just minutes from downtown Phoenix, the Desert Botanical Garden covers 140 acres, with over 50,000 plants on display. Several trails wind through the main areas of the gardens, including the **Desert Wildflower Loop Trail,** the **Desert Discovery Loop Trail,** the **Center for Desert Living Trail,** the **Sonoran Desert Nature Loop Trail,** and the **Plans & People of the Sonoran Desert Loop Trail.** There's also a lovely gift shop, seasonal plant sales, and two on-site dining options. Special events include the **Electric Desert Light and Sound Experience, Las Noches de las Luminarias,** and the **Music in the Garden Concert Series.**

5 Tohono Chul Botanical Gardens & Galleries

7366 N. Paseo del Norte, Tucson, AZ 85704; 520-742-6455
tohonochul.org

While the Arizona–Sonora Desert Museum (see page 112) gets most of the attention in Tucson, Tohono Chul is well worth a visit. Covering 49 acres on the north side of Tucson, Tohono Chul has several themed gardens, including a **Hummingbird Garden, Penstemon Garden, Desert Palm Oasis,** and **Children's Garden.** Daily tours are offered, with topics ranging from birds to art to butterflies, and more. Eco Stations are set up from October through April, where visitors can learn more about the plants and animals of the Sonoran Desert. Don't miss the gift shops and art galleries before ending your visit with a delicious meal at the **Garden Bistro.** There are many special events and tours, and if you're visiting in the summer, keep an eye out for **Bloom Night**—the single night each year when the Arizona Queen of the Night (*Peniocereus greggii*) blooms. It's a major event that draws crowds to see the world's largest collection of this unique flower.

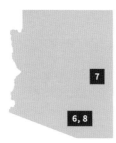

6 Tucson Botanical Gardens

2150 N. Alvernon Way, Tucson, AZ 85712; 520-326-9686
tucsonbotanical.org

Tucson Botanical Gardens has 17 specialty gardens spanning 5.5 acres, right in the heart of Tucson. The specialty gardens include an herb garden, a pollinator garden, a cactus and succulent garden, a xeriscape garden, and a Native American crops garden. From October to May, visit the **Butterfly & Orchid Pavilion,** a lush tropical greenhouse with butterflies from all over the world. The gardens are well shaded, so even a summer visit is enjoyable. (Bring water!) Children will love the model train garden and the recently renovated **Children's Discovery Garden.** Save time for a bite at **Café Botanica,** which features local, sustainable ingredients, including herbs and vegetables straight from the on-site gardens. Tucson Botanical Gardens has a calendar full of festive events, as well as classes and special tours.

7 White Mountain Nature Center

425 Woodland Road, Lakeside, AZ 85929; 928-358-3069
whitemountainnaturecenter.org

In the high country of the White Mountains, the White Mountain Nature Center sits on 10 acres in the resort town of Lakeside. Most of your time at the center will be spent outdoors on the hiking paths, which link into the adjacent **Big Springs Environmental Study Area.** The interpretive trails are a great place to learn about the local flora and fauna, and the center has a full calendar of events, demonstrations, classes, and camps.

8 Yume Japanese Gardens

2130 N. Alvernon Way, Tucson, AZ 85712; 520-272-3200
yumegardens.org

I always find Japanese gardens to be such relaxing places, and this one in Tucson is no exception. The intimate space includes several koi ponds and teahouse models, and the on-site museum includes Japanese art and an impressive calendar of classes and events, such as calligraphy and origami instruction. Perhaps the most impressive aspect of these gardens is their ability to create such a tranquil environment in the heart of the city. Open Thursday–Sunday in season; closed May 5–October 5; Thanksgiving week; December 24, 25, and 31; and January 1.

Arizona Sonora Desert Museum, Tucson, AZ

Queen Mine, Bisbee, AZ

ARIZONA IS A ROCK HOUND'S PARADISE. From brilliant turquoise stones sourced from quarries across the state to abandoned silver and gold mines that once thrived, it's no coincidence that Arizona is home to the largest gem and mineral show in the United States (see "Festivals," page 132).

SCIENCE & NATURE:
Rocks & Minerals

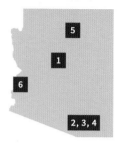

1 Arizona Copper Art Museum

849 Main St., Clarkdale, AZ 86324; 928-649-1858
copperartmuseum.com

Arizona is the leading producer of copper in the United States, so when the Meinke family of Minnesota started looking for a public home for their copper collection, the town of Clarkdale seemed a perfect fit. Clarkdale was founded as a company smelter town for the United Verde Copper Company in Jerome. The museum, housed in the 1927 Clarkdale High School building, features an extensive copper collection. Collections are grouped into several classrooms by category, which includes kitchenware, drinkware, distillery, winery, religious art, and military art.

2 ASARCO Mineral Discovery Center

1421 W. Pima Mine Road, Sahuarita, AZ 85629; 520-625-7513
asarco.com/about-us/our-locations/asarco-mineral-discovery-center

It's not every day that you get to tour a fully operational open-pit mine. The American Smelting and Refining Company (ASARCO) operates several copper mines in the United States, including the Mission Mine in Sahuarita, just south of Tucson. Get an up-close view of how copper ore is mined, then go indoors to see how it's processed into the final product. The Discovery Center is open six days a week and free of charge. Tours are offered on Saturdays only for a small fee; they're given on an air-conditioned bus, so it's appropriate for all ages. Don't miss all of the copper crafts in the gift shop before you leave.

3 Colossal Cave Mountain Park

16721 E. Old Spanish Trail Road, Vail, AZ 85641; 520-647-7275
colossalcave.com

This Pima County park has cave tours and much more. Set on 2,400 acres, the park is on the National Register of Historic Places and much of the buildings and walkways were built by the Civilian Conservation Corps in the 1930s. Colossal Cave is a dry, or dormant, cave, meaning that water is no longer flowing and creating formations inside. (Head to nearby **Kartchner Caverns** for an example of a wet cave; see below.) The **Classic Cave Tour** is held every hour, and if you're feeling adventurous, there is a **Ladder Tour** and **Intermediate and Advanced Wild Cave Tours**. The Classic Cave Tour covers 0.75 mile and more than 300 steps, so wear good shoes. Elsewhere in the park, there are hiking trails, horseback riding, a petting zoo, and a primitive campground. Check the website for special events, such as a saguaro fruit harvest with the Tohono O'odham at the end of June.

4 Kartchner Caverns State Park

2980 AZ 90, Benson, AZ 85602; 520-586-4100
azstateparks.com/kartchner

One of the most pristine public caves I've ever visited, Kartchner Caverns are unique in that they were not discovered until 1974 and not opened to the public until 2003. Other famous caves have been used by humans for centuries, and the features get degraded over time. This is not the case at Kartchner Caverns, and you'll see why on your visit. They are very strict about what can go in the cave and how the tours are led. Make sure to reserve your tours online ahead of time as they do sell out, especially during peak seasons; some last-minute tours are added in the morning. Aboveground, the park has hiking trails, wildlife viewing, camping, and cabins for rent.

5 Moenave Dinosaur Tracks

US 160, Tuba City, AZ 86045

East of the Grand Canyon on the Navajo Reservation, near the Cameron Trading Post and Tuba City, there are dinosaur tracks and other fossils embedded in a dry riverbed. At present this is just a small roadside attraction manned by local Navajos; bring cash for a small tip, as they will guide you to the tracks and give you a short tour that also includes dinosaur egg fossils, bones, and petroglyphs. Several vendors also usually set up near the tracks to sell Native American crafts and jewelry.

6 Quartzsite

Quartzsite, AZ 85346
quartzsiteaz.org

The town of Quartzsite has acquired a few monikers over the years. In addition to being the "boondocking capital of the US," it's also the self-proclaimed "rock capital of the world." The months of January and February see this dusty Western Arizona town transformed into a giant swap meet for rockhounds and gem collectors. Rockhounds have been

7

scouring the desert surrounding Quartzsite for decades, with various deposits producing agate, petrified wood, and turquoise, along with geodes at the **Hauser Geode Beds,** about 60 miles west in California.

7 Queen Mine

47 N. Dart Road, Bisbee, AZ 85603; 520-432-2071
queenminetour.com

Bisbee is one of Arizona's best mining towns, and the Queen Mine is what started it all. One of the largest, most profitable, and longest-running copper mines in the world, until it closed in 1975, Queen Mine didn't stay closed for long, opening for tours in 1976. As you don your hard hat and vest, you might think you're in for a cheesy attraction, but it's actually a very educational and interesting tour. All of the tour guides are retired employees from the mine, so they actually worked these tunnels and have a wealth of knowledge and stories to share. The tour takes you on a railroad track 1,500 feet into the mine, and there's quite a bit of walking as well.

Arizona Copper Art Museum, Clarkdale, AZ

Biosphere 2, Oracle, AZ

WITH SEVERAL WORLD-CLASS universities in Arizona, science is a hot topic in the state. These science museums are sure to educate and entertain, whether you're a budding scientist or enthusiastic amateur. The science-and-discovery theme continues into the Stargazing chapter (see page 126).

SCIENCE & NATURE:
Science Museums

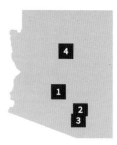

1 Arizona Science Center

600 E. Washington St., Phoenix, AZ 85004; 602-716-2000
azscience.org

The Arizona Science Center's mission is to inspire, educate and engage curious minds through science. With a convenient location in Phoenix's Heritage Park campus downtown, it's a great place for families to escape the desert heat for a few hours. More than 350 hands-on activities and live demos are spread across four levels. Exhibits include **Forces of Nature** (a 4-D weather experience), a bug collection, the **Body Depot,** and an outdoor atrium with water play. Special exhibits, which require an additional entry fee, include planetarium presentations, laser light shows, and a 3-D movie theater. Next door is **CREATE Makerspace,** a new addition to the science center that hosts workshops in 3-D printing, laser cutting, woodworking, and sewing. Check the website for special events and programs.

2 Biosphere 2

32540 S. Biosphere Road, Oracle, AZ 85623; 520-621-4800
biosphere2.org

This scientific center north of Tucson has a fascinating history in addition to ongoing research and experiments. Construction began in 1986 to study self-sustaining space-colonization technology. In the early 1990s, eight humans were locked inside for two years, along with chickens, goats, and pigs. Although the human missions were discontinued, research continues today. On a tour of the facility, you'll see the space where the participants lived, and you'll visit many wilderness environments including a rainforest, savanna, desert, and ocean. The **Landscape Evolution Observatory** is the largest geological project in the world; here, scientists can accelerate the impact of rising carbon levels in the atmosphere and study how our planet works in the face of climate change. Guided tours are ongoing throughout the day; plan to spend a few hours for the tour, visitor center, gift shop, and café.

3 Flandrau Science Center

1601 E. University Blvd., Tucson, AZ 85721; 520-621-4516
flandrau.org

This science center on the University of Arizona campus feels like several museums in one. Exhibits include the **UA Mineral Museum, The Fossil Corner,** and a special display on sharks. The planetarium is one-of-a-kind, with a full-dome projection system that allows visitors to see the aspects of our solar system and beyond, up close and personal. The planetarium theater has multiples shows each day, from kid-friendly educational movies to laser light shows featuring the music of Queen and Pink Floyd.

4 US Geological Survey Flagstaff Science Campus

2255 N. Gemini Drive, Flagstaff, AZ 86001; 928-556-7000
arizona.usgs.gov

The Flagstaff region played a major scientific role in the Apollo moon missions, including astronaut training, instrument development, and lunar mapping. Every astronaut who walked on the moon between 1963 and 1972 trained in Flagstaff. At the USGS Flagstaff Science Campus, visitors to Building 6, the **Shoemaker Astrogeology Science Center,** can see **Grover,** a geologic rover that was used to train astronauts for moon missions. (If you have time, drive out to the **Cinder Lakes Crater Field,** where the volcanic soil was blasted to mirror the landscape of the moon!) Other buildings in the USGS Science Campus include the **Powell Building of Geology, Hydrology, and Geography,** as well as the **Southwest Biological Science Center** in the Dutton Building. Note that these are working offices, so plan a self-guided tour using materials provided online.

Rosette Mosaic

ARIZONA IS HOME TO more certified Dark Sky Places than any other state in the country, and Tucson is home to the International Dark Sky Association. Arizona even has a residential community—**Arizona Sky Village**—developed specifically for astronomers, where nearly every home has its own domed observatory and outdoor lights are forbidden! Stargazing is serious business here in Arizona, and it's one of the things I love most about living here. In addition to the places listed in this book, many local parks departments have stargazing nights, so be sure to ask at the parks' visitor centers.

SCIENCE & NATURE:
Stargazing

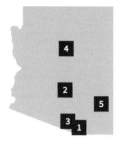

1 Fred Lawrence Whipple Observatory

670 Mount Hopkins Road, Amado, AZ 85645; 520-879-4407
cfa.harvard.edu/flwo

Affiliated with the Smithsonian Institution and Harvard University, this observatory just north of Tubac includes a visitor center and seasonal tours. Start your trip at the visitor center, which includes several exhibits about astronomy and astrophysics as well as some smaller telescopes and hiking trails outside. Ideally, you should visit in the fall or spring, when tours are offered. The tour is an all-day affair starting in the morning at the visitor center, followed by a bus ride up the winding mountain road to view the telescopes up close. The tour returns to the visitor center in the late afternoon. Reservations are required. Additional events, including star parties and lectures, are in the works for the future, so check online for the latest details.

2 Gilbert Rotary Centennial Observatory

2757 E. Guadalupe Road, Gilbert, AZ 85234
grcoonline.org

From the Phoenix area, it's not always easy to plan a trip up a remote mountain to look at the stars, especially if you have kids in tow. The Gilbert Rotary Centennial Observatory is the perfect spot for stargazing in the Valley, and you don't have to go driving a bunch of crazy roads after dark. The location, at the Gilbert Riparian Preserve, is dark enough for urban stargazing but close enough that you can be back at your Phoenix hotel in 30 minutes. Stargazing events are held every Friday and Saturday evening for a suggested donation of $5; other events, such as star parties and lectures, are scheduled occasionally throughout the year. This is a great opportunity to see planets and constellations through an eyepiece.

3 Kitt Peak National Observatory

AZ 386, 11 miles south of the junction with AZ 86 (West Tucson–Ajo Highway), Tucson, AZ 85726; 520-318-8000
noao.edu/kpno

Kitt Peak, the second-highest peak on the Tohono O'odham Indian Reservation, sports an impressive array of telescopes, including the world's largest solar telescope. The main attraction are the evening programs, but the daytime activities also warrant a visit. Daytime programs include docent-led tours and solar viewing. The nightly observing program is very popular and does sell out in advance, so reservations are required. The program starts before sunrise with a light dinner and a recorded program before guests head outside to watch the sun set. After dark, participants take turns at different telescopes and the evening concludes with identifying constellations with binoculars and star charts. They also offer more in-depth programs, such as a dark-sky discovery program and astrophotography programs.

4 Lowell Observatory

1400 W. Mars Hill Road, Flagstaff, AZ 86001; 928-774-3358
lowell.edu

Unlike many Arizona observatories which are set far outside of town in remote locations, Lowell Observatory is right in Flagstaff, so there's no reason not to visit "the home of Pluto." That's right—the planet/not-a-planet Pluto was discovered here in 1930. This is only one facet of Flagstaff's rich lunar legacy, which includes the prestige of being the world's first International Dark Sky City. Lowell Observatory has presentations on the hour, and telescopes are open for viewing when the skies are clear. Special events include Q&A sessions with educators, a preschool camp for kids, and guest speakers. Even under cloudy skies, the presentations and exhibits make Lowell Observatory worth a visit.

5 Mount Graham International Observatory

1480 AZ 366, Safford, AZ 85546; 928-428-2739
mgio.arizona.edu

Mount Graham International Observatory is one of the best in the world, thanks to a remote location and lack of nearby light pollution. Tours of the site are given on weekends from mid-May to mid-October, where visitors can get a closeup look at the three main telescopes: The **Vatican Advanced Technology Telescope,** locally referred to as "the Pope's telescope" and operated in cooperation with the Vatican Observatory; the **Large Binocular Telescope,** one of the world's most powerful optical telescopes; and the **Heinrich Hertz Telescope.** Reservations are required for the tours. At the base of the mountain, make sure to visit the **Discovery Park Campus,** where they have stargazing events and a space shuttle simulator.

8 Various locations

6 Mount Lemmon SkyCenter

9800 E. Ski Run Road, Mount Lemmon, AZ 85619; 520-626-8122
skycenter.arizona.edu

Mount Lemmon SkyCenter lays claim to having the largest telescope that the public is able to use. Access to the SkyCenter requires a reservation, so don't drive to the top of Mount Lemmon without one. The **SkyNights** stargazing program is the main way to experience the SkyCenter, and with limited capacity, spots tend to fill up quickly. The 5-hour program starts with a spectacular sunset over Oro Valley before heading inside for dinner and a presentation. Afterwards, guests visit two of the telescopes on property and check out various stars, planets, and constellations. Daytime tours are available for groups of 20 or more.

7 Patterson Observatory

1140 N. Colombo Ave., Sierra Vista, AZ 85635; 520-458-8278
universitysouthfoundation.com/patterson-observatory

In partnership with the University South Foundation, the Huachuca Astronomy Club operates a visitor center at this observatory next to Cochise College. The public viewings are free and run by volunteers with their own equipment, but they are scheduled only once per month and heavily dependent on good weather and clear skies. The current schedule calls for events on the Thursday nearest the first quarter moon; check online for the latest information and any updates on weather cancellations. This is a great volunteer event for the Sierra Vista area, if you happen to be in the right place at the right time.

8 | International Dark Sky Parks

Various locations statewide

The following locations have been designated as International Dark Sky Parks by the International Dark Sky Association (darksky.org), which means they're all excellent places to view the night sky.

- **Grand Canyon National Park** nps.gov/grca
- **Kartchner Caverns State Park** azstateparks.com/kartchner
- **Oracle State Park** azstateparks.com/oracle
- **Parashant National Monument** nps.gov/para
- **Petrified Forest National Park** nps.gov/pefo
- **Sunset Crater Volcano National Monument** nps.gov/sucr
- **Tumacácori National Historical Park** nps.gov/tuma
- **Tonto National Monument** nps.gov/tont
- **Walnut Canyon National Monument** nps.gov/waca
- **Wupatki National Monument** nps.gov/wupa

Havasu Balloon Festival and Fair, Lake Havasu City, AZ

FROM TACOS TO RODEOS, there's always a festival going on in Arizona. In the summer, we need a distraction to take our minds off the heat, and come winter, we look for any excuse to celebrate! Rodeos and Native celebrations are a big deal in Arizona, and you'll find plenty of both throughout the state.

UNIQUELY ARIZONA:
Festivals

133

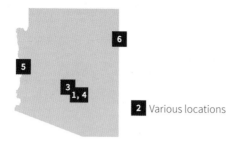

2 Various locations

1 Arizona Renaissance Festival (February–March)

12601 E. US Highway 60, Gold Canyon, AZ 85118; 520-463-2600
arizona.renfestinfo.com

For eight weekends in February and March, the Renaissance Festival brings medieval entertainment to Arizona. This permanent site has 14 stages spread over 30 acres of land east of Mesa, Arizona. Each weekend has a theme, such as Pirate Invasion, Celtic Weekend, and Time Traveler Weekend. Costumes are optional, and you can rent them on-site if you want to blend in. Visitors are treated to everything from falconry, pirates, musical performances, and a medieval arts-and-crafts fair. The three daily jousts are a festival highlight; get to the arena a bit early for a good seat. Make sure you bring a hat or umbrella, sunscreen, and cash for the vendors. Look around online to find out where discounted tickets are sold.

2 Arizona Restaurant Week (May/September)

Throughout Central and Southern Arizona; 602-307-9134
arizonarestaurantweek.com

This fun event happens twice a year, in May and September. More than 100 participating restaurants in Central and Southern Arizona offer prix fixe dinners for $34 or $44, allowing foodie travelers to try a whole host of new restaurants around the state. The venues range from casual to fine dining, with nearly every type of cuisine represented.

3 Arizona Taco Festival (October)

Salt River Fields, 7555 N. Pima Road, Scottsdale, AZ 85258; 480-270-5000
aztacofestival.com

Some people think I moved to Arizona for the tacos. They aren't wrong. Sharing a border with Sonora, Mexico, means nothing but good things for Arizona cuisine, and 2019 marks the 10th year of the Arizona Taco Festival, held in Scottsdale each October. More than

50 restaurants and food trucks serve up $2 tacos in traditional and creative flavor combinations. While you eat, enjoy live music, *lucha libre* pro wrestling, eating contests, a Chihuahua beauty pageant, and cooking classes. A general admission ticket is required, and you purchase tokens to pay at the various food stalls. There's also a tequila expo with over 100 brands of tequila, available in half-ounce samples with an admission ticket. Bring your fat pants and your designated driver!

4 Country Thunder Music Festival (April)

20585 E. Water Way, Florence, AZ 85132; 866-388-0007
countrythunder.com/az

The hippies have Woodstock, the millennials have Bonnaroo, and country music fans have Country Thunder. Held in Arizona since 1996, this music festival includes four full days of performances spread across three main stages. Prior year headliners include Trace Adkins, Jason Aldean, Luke Bryan, and Tim McGraw. The festival takes place in Florence, about an hour southeast of Phoenix. On-site camping is available, with tent rentals and glamping for a true "luxury festival" experience.

5 Havasu Balloon Festival and Fair (January)

Lake Havasu State Park, 171 London Bridge Road, Lake Havasu City, AZ 86403; 928-505-2440
havasuballoonfest.com

January is the best time to visit the hottest city in the United States. The Havasu Balloon Festival and Fair has become the largest January balloon festival in the country, and the setting is spectacular. With over 70 hot-air balloons plus food, entertainment, and rides, this four-day event is worth the trip to Lake Havasu City. During the day, stake out a spot along the lakeshore or join a boat cruise to watch from the water. Balloon pilots do a "splash and dash" near the London Bridge; crowds gather early for a good spot. At night, don't miss the balloon glow as the sun goes down.

6 Navajo Nation Fair (September)

Navajo Nation Fairgrounds, AZ 264 at Lagoon Road, Window Rock, AZ 86515; 928-871-6478
facebook.com/navajonationfair

Kicking off on Labor Day and lasting through the following weekend, the Navajo Nation Fair aims to "preserve and promote pride in the Navajo heritage and culture for the benefit of the Navajo Nation." Participants and spectators come from all over the Navajo Nation and beyond to experience arts and crafts, 4-H shows, horse racing, footraces, parades, powwows, Indian and junior rodeos, and the

Festivals

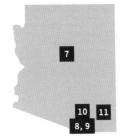

 12 Various locations

Miss Navajo Nation pageant. This is a great place to try traditional Navajo dishes such as fry bread and mutton stew. Carnivals and daily concerts round out a very full week of fun. Check the schedule online for specific events and demonstrations.

7 Sedona International Film Festival (February)

Mary D. Fisher Theatre, 2030 W. AZ 89A, Sedona, AZ 86336; 928-282-1177
sedonafilmfestival.com

For more than 25 years, the Sedona International Film Festival has been drawing filmmakers and film fanatics to Sedona. The nine-day event includes over 150 films; documentaries, short films, animation, foreign films, and feature films are all represented. Attendees can choose from multiple ticket packages, from a Priority Pass that includes every screening to individual tickets available one week before the festival begins.

8 Tubac Festival of the Arts (February)

Tubac, AZ; 520-398-2704
tubacaz.com/tubac-festivals

Tubac is all about art and artists year-round, but come February, the Festival of the Arts fills the streets and the shops with art. Southern Arizona's longest running art festival is an easy day trip from Tucson, or a good excuse to stay overnight in Tubac. This juried event showcases local and visiting artists, with everything on offer from traditional art to jewelry, artisan foods, and home decor. In addition to the excellent restaurants in Tubac, street food is another highlight of the Festival of the Arts.

9 Tucson Gem Show (February/September)

Citywide; 877-GEM-SHOW (436-7469)
jogsshow.com

Tucson's biggest event has gotten so big that they've added a round of fall shows in addition to the usual winter show. The Tucson Gem Show takes over the town, with nearly 50 different shows taking place around the city. From small dealers in motel rooms to huge exhibits at the Tucson Convention Center, there's something for everyone. Planning your first trip can be overwhelming, but there's an app for that: the **Official Tucson Gem Show Guide** (iOS and Android). While many shows are open to the public, some are wholesale-only and require a business license and taxpayer ID; the app or website can help you filter out the wholesale shows if you're just a casual buyer or browser.

10 Tucson Jazz Festival (January)

Multiple venues, Tucson, AZ; 520-428-4853
tucsonjazzfestival.org

For 10 days in January, world-class jazz musicians descend on Tucson for performances across the city. Past performers have included Kristin Chenoweth, Trombone Shorty, and Bobby McFerrin. Performances take place at several venues, including the Fox Tucson Theatre, Club Congress, Centennial Hall, and Tucson Music Hall. The festival culminates with the all-day Downtown Jazz Fiesta, a free event featuring two outdoor stages.

11 Willcox Wine Country Festival (October)

157 N. Railroad Avenue, Willcox, AZ 85643
willcoxwinecountry.org/event/willcox-wine-festival

You can plan your own Willcox Wine Country tour (see page 147) and drive to all of the amazing tasting rooms, or you can catch them all in one place in October. Nearly 20 wineries participate in this annual festival alongside many arts-and-crafts vendors, food trucks, and live music. Although you must be 21 to drink, the event is family-friendly, and you'll want to take advantage of your visit to stay overnight and explore the Willcox area, which includes **Chiricahua National Monument** nearby (see page 73). In 2013 *Fodor's* listed this event among its top 10 fall wine festivals in the US.

12 Rodeos

Statewide

Rodeos are a big deal in Arizona and you'll find them year-round all over the state. Tucson schools even break for Rodeo Week. Prescott lays claim to the world's oldest rodeo, while Payson claims to be the oldest continuous rodeo. Rodeos also play a big part in the Native culture, so each group has at least one annual rodeo. Here's a sampling of the rodeos you'll find throughout the state.

JANUARY
Tohono O'odham Nation Rodeo & Fair
Eugene P. Tashquinth Sr. Livestock Complex, AZ 86, Sells, AZ; 520-383-2588
tonation-nsn.gov

FEBRUARY
Tucson Rodeo
4823 S. Sixth Ave., Tucson, AZ 85714; 520-955-8887
tucsonrodeo.com

MARCH
Cave Creek Rodeo Days
Cave Creek Memorial Arena, 37201 N. 28th St., Cave Creek, AZ; 480-304-5634
cavecreekrodeo.com

MAY
Kayenta Rodeo
Kayenta Rodeo Ground, Indian Route 591 (0.8 mile south of US 160), Kayenta, AZ;
928-409-9329
kayentarodeo.com

JUNE
Flagstaff Rodeo
Fort Tuthill County Park, 2446 Fort Tuthill Loop, Flagstaff, AZ; 928-707-1119
flagstaffrodeo.com

JULY
Prescott Frontier Days
840 Rodeo Drive, Prescott, AZ; 928-445-3103
worldsoldestrodeo.com

AUGUST
Payson Pro Rodeo
Payson Event Center, 1400 S. Beeline Highway, Payson, AZ; 928-978-0694
paysonprorodeo.com

White Mountain Apache Tribal Fair & Rodeo
Whiteriver Fairgrounds, 143 Fairground Road, Whiteriver, AZ; 928-338-2492
wmatfair.com

SEPTEMBER
Andy Devine Days Rodeo
Mohave County Fairgrounds, 2600 Fairgrounds Blvd., Kingman, AZ; 928-753-2636
kingsmenrodeo.org

Bareback riding event during the Tohono O'odham Nation Rodeo

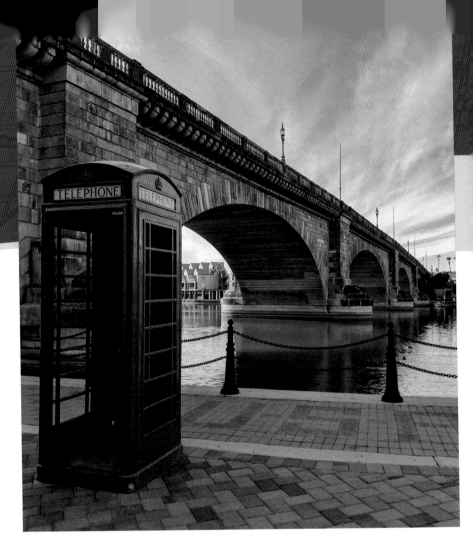

The London Bridge, Lake Havasu City, AZ

THIS CHAPTER COVERS everything that defies a category—whether it's a mysterious natural phenomenon or a quirky roadside attraction that's worth a quick detour on your day trips around Arizona.

ODDS & ENDS:
Unusual Arizona

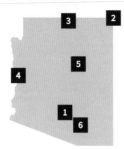

1 Casa Grande Neon Sign Park

408 N. Sacaton St., Casa Grande, AZ 85122; 520-836-8744
neonsignpark.com

A fun place to stretch your legs on the drive between Phoenix and Tucson, the Casa Grande Main Street organization has created this outdoor space containing several tailgate benches and 14 vintage and neon signs from Casa Grande's past. Plaques tell the story of the signs, helping visitors picture the businesses of Casa Grande in the 1950s.

2 Four Corners Monument

597 NM 597, Teec Nos Pos, AZ 86514; 928-206-2540
utah.com/four-corners

Not far from Monument Valley, the Four Corners Monument is the only place in the US where four states intersect at one point. Using both hands and feet, you can technically be in four states at the same time. Four Corners is on Navajo land, and they operate a small gift shop and visitor center on-site. Sure, it's a bit gimmicky, but if it's not too far out of the way, it's worth a quick stop for the photo opportunity.

3 Horseshoe Bend

US 89 between Mile Markers 544 and 545, Page, AZ
horseshoebend.com

Just south of Page, the Colorado River bends in a most dramatic fashion. The result is a spectacular overlook area that has been photographed thousands, if not millions, of times. In fact, in 2017 a major overhaul was started to handle the massive increase in traffic: what used to be a small dirt parking lot off the road is now a full parking lot with an admission fee. You can also take a shuttle from nearby Page. I recommend going early in the morning to beat the crowds. The hike to the overlook is only 0.75 mile, and they're in the process of making this accessible as well as adding guardrails—it's currently a 1,000-foot drop to the river with no protection.

4 London Bridge

1340 McCulloch Blvd., Lake Havasu City, AZ 86403; 928-855-5655
golakehavasu.com/london-bridge

Lake Havasu City has a quirky history that includes acquisition of the London Bridge in 1968 by the city's founder. The bridge originally spanned the Thames River from 1831 to 1968, although some of the granite used in the bridge dates all the way back to the 13th century. Robert McCulloch, of McCulloch chainsaw fame, purchased the bridge for $2.4 million and had it disassembled, shipped via the Panama Canal, and reassembled in Lake Havasu City. The bridge was built over an isthmus leading to a peninsula. After construction, the soil below the bridge was dug out, creating a river channel to flow under the bridge and creating what is now Lake Havasu City's Island District. The London Bridge remains in *The Guinness Book of World Records* as the largest antique ever sold. The Visitor Center offers a 90-minute walking tour several times a week.

5 Meteor Crater

I-40 Exit 233, Winslow, AZ 86047; 928-289-5898
meteorcrater.com

As you're traveling between Flagstaff and Winslow on I-40, don't miss the chance to see the best and most perfectly preserved impact crater on Earth. Nearly 200 impact craters have been identified on our planet, but this location is where the mystery of impact craters was solved. Made by a meteorite 50,000 years ago, the crater is 700 feet deep and more than 4,000 feet across. The Apollo astronauts trained at the site from 1964 to 1972, and astronauts still train here today. Every hour and half hour, a 10-minute movie plays in the theater, and a 45-minute rim tour is available every hour. While pets are not permitted in the visitor center, air-conditioned kennels are available. There's also a Subway restaurant on-site, as well as a gift shop with all kinds of Route 66 and geology souvenirs.

6 The Mini Time Machine Museum of Miniatures

4455 E. Camp Lowell Drive, Tucson, Arizona 85712; 520-881-0606
theminitimemachine.org

This Tucson museum is dedicated to "preserving and advancing the art of miniatures." I didn't even know there *was* an "art of miniatures," but The Mini Time Museum is fascinating. You won't believe the level of detail in each of these miniatures. The museum has several sections, each interesting and unique. The **Enchanted Realm Gallery** contains

fantasy themed miniatures and collectibles like pocket dragons and Kewpie dolls. **Exploring the World** showcases cultures from around the world, including Thai spirit houses and a 14-room Rococo château. The **History Gallery** shows glimpses of 18th-through early-20th-century life, including the 25-room Lagniappe, a Mount Vernon–inspired miniature mansion.

7 Sedona Vortexes

Sedona, AZ
sedona.net/vortex

Part of the allure of Sedona for metaphysical travelers and artists are the vortexes scattered around the surrounding desert. A vortex is a place where special energy is said to radiate from or into the earth, and those so inclined are able to sense this vortex. Four specific sites around Sedona have been identified as vortexes: **Bell Rock, Cathedral Rock, Boynton Canyon,** and **Airport Mesa.** Tour operators around town can take you on a vortex tour, or you can go out and explore them on your own. Pop into any of the shops selling crystals, and you'll get all the info you need about the vortexes.

Unusual
Arizona

Charron Vineyards, Vail, AZ

PERHAPS THE BIGGEST SURPRISE for me when I moved to Arizona was learning that anything can grow here, especially grapes! As it turns out, thanks to the miracle of irrigation, there's actually a lot that grows in Arizona—in fact, it's estimated that nearly 100% of the lettuce consumed in the winter months in the United States is grown in **Yuma**, where seasonal agricultural tours are available. Arizona also has three grape-growing regions, two of which are certified official American Viticultural Areas (AVA): **Sonoita** in Santa Cruz County, **Willcox** in Cochise County, and the **Verde Valley** in Yavapai County.

A TASTE OF ARIZONA:
Orchards, Vineyards & Wineries

ORCHARDS

Apple Annie's Orchard
2081 W. Hardy Road, Willcox, AZ 85643; 520-384-2084
appleannies.com

Dateland Date Gardens
1737 S. Avenue 64 E., Dateland, AZ 85333; 928-454-2772
dateland.com

Queen Creek Olive Mill
25062 S. Meridian Road, Queen Creek, AZ 85142; 480-888-9290
queencreekolivemill.com

VINEYARDS & WINERIES

Arizona Hops and Vines
3450 AZ 82, Sonoita, AZ 85637; 301-237-6556
azhopsandvines.com

Charron Vineyards & Winery
18585 S. Sonoita Highway, Vail, AZ 85641; 520-762-8585
charronvineyards.com

Page Springs Cellars
1500 N. Page Springs Road, Cornville, AZ 86325; 928-639-3004
pagespringscellars.com

Rancho Rossa Vineyards
201 Cattle Ranch Lane, Elgin, AZ 85611; 520-455-0700
ranchorossa.com

Verde Valley Wine Trail
Features 24 wineries in the Verde Valley; see website below for map
vvwinetrail.com

Wines of Willcox
Represents 18 wineries; see website below for maps
willcoxwines.com

Index

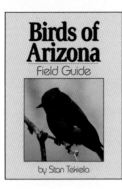

Birds of Arizona

Stan Tekiela

**ISBN: 978-1-59193-015-0 • $14.95 • 4.38 x 6
paperback • 364 pages • full color**

Learn to Identify Birds in Arizona!

Make bird watching in Arizona even more enjoyable! With Stan Tekiela's famous field guide, bird identification is simple and informative. There's no need to look through dozens of photos of birds that don't live in your area. This book features 145 species of Arizona birds, organized by color for ease of use. Do you see a yellow bird and don't know what it is? Go to the yellow section to find out. Fact-filled information, a compare feature, range maps, and detailed photographs help to ensure that you positively identify the birds that you see.

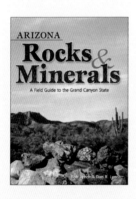

Arizona Rocks & Minerals

Bob Lynch & Dan R. Lynch

**ISBN: 978-1-59193-237-6 • $14.95 • 4.38 x 6
paperback • 252 pages • full color**

Your Must-Have Guide to Arizona's Rocks and Minerals!

Get the perfect guide to rocks and minerals in the Grand Canyon State! This book by Bob Lynch and Dan R. Lynch features comprehensive entries for 106 Arizona rocks and minerals, from common rocks to rare finds. Learn from the fascinating information about everything from agates and copper to turquoise and gold. The easy-to-use format means you'll quickly find what you need to know and where to look. The authors' incredible, sharp, full-color photographs depict the detail needed for identification—no need to guess from line drawings. Identifying and collecting is fun and informative with this field guide.

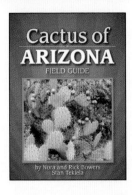

Cactus of Arizona

Nora and Rick Bowers, Stan Tekiela

**ISBN: 978-1-59193-068-6 • $14.95 • 4.38 x 6
paperback • 236 pages • full color**

Learn to Identify Cacti in Arizona!

Learn about and identify cacti in Arizona with this famous field guide to 50 of the state's species. Organized by family, then by shape, the book by Nora Bowers, Rick Bowers, and Stan Tekiela gives you all the details needed to positively identify each cactus. Do you see a species and don't know what it is? Use the shape icons to narrow your search. From there, you'll find more photos per cactus than any other field guide, making visual identification quick and easy. Range maps and close-ups of spines, flowers, and fruit further aid in identification. With full-page pictures, detailed descriptions, and fascinating natural history, this is the best guide to Arizona's cacti!

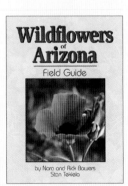

Wildflowers of Arizona

Stan Tekiela

**ISBN: 978-1-59193-069-3 • $16.95 • 4.38 x 6
paperback • 432 pages • full color**

Learn to Identify Wildflowers in Arizona!

You've seen Arizona's beautiful wildflowers. Now learn to identify them. This is your field guide to 200 of Arizona's wildflowers. Full-page photographs and an easy-to-read format present the information that's critical to accurate identification. And the species are organized by color, so when you see a purple flower, simply turn to the purple section of the book. Wildflower identification has never been easier!

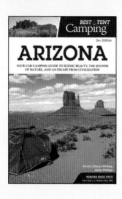

Best Tent Camping: Arizona

Kirstin Olmon Phillips, Kelly Phillips

ISBN: 978-1-63404-076-1 • **$16.95** • **6 x 9**
paperback • **192 pages** • **full color** • **2nd edition**

Perfect Camping for You in Arizona!

The Grand Canyon State provides a spectacular backdrop for some of the most scenic campgrounds in the country, from the cool forests of the Mongollon Rim and the White Mountains to the verdant crowns of southern Arizona's sky islands. But do you know which campgrounds offer the most privacy? Which are the best for first-time campers? Kirstin Olmon Phillips and Kelly Phillips have traversed the entire state and compiled the most up-to-date research to steer you to the perfect spot!

Best Tent Camping: Arizona presents 50 national park, state park, and recreation site campgrounds, organized into five distinct regions. Selections are based on location, topography, size, and overall appeal, and every site is rated for beauty, privacy, spaciousness, safety and security, and cleanliness—so you'll always know what to expect. The new full-color edition of this proven guidebook provides everything you need to know, with detailed maps of each campground and key information such as fees, restrictions, dates of operation, and facilities, as well as driving directions and GPS coordinates.

Whether you seek a quiet campground near a fish-filled stream or a family campground with all the amenities, grab *Best Tent Camping: Arizona*. It's an escape for all who wish to find those special locales that recharge the mind, body, and spirit. This guide is a keeper.

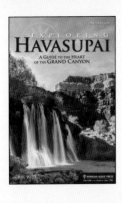

Exploring Havasupai

Greg Witt

ISBN: 978-1-63404-070-9 • **$19.95** • **6 x 9**
paperback • **144 pages** • **full color** • **2nd edition**

Your Guide to Paradise!

Deep in the Grand Canyon lies a place of unmatched beauty—a place where blue-green water cascades over fern-clad cliffs into travertine pools, where great blue heron skim canyon streams, and where giant cottonwoods and graceful willows thrive in the shade of majestic sandstone cliffs. Havasupai is a paradise enveloped in one of the earth's most rugged and parched landscapes.

Exploring Havasupai by author Greg Witt is the essential destination guide for those visiting the area. The updated guidebook is filled with insider tips, fascinating background, and essential information. It identifies many new hikes, mines, springs, and historical sites never before revealed in a Grand Canyon or Havasupai guidebook. Details on canyon geology, weather patterns, and the unique flora and fauna add depth to a hiker's experience.

Exploring Havasupai includes detailed maps, trail descriptions, stunning full-color photographs, and intriguing historical insights. This is the must-have guide for canyon visitors, whether they are arriving by helicopter, on horseback, or on foot.

60 Hikes Within 60 Miles: Phoenix

Charles Liu

**ISBN: 978-1-63404-074-7 • $18.95 • 6 x 9
paperback • 336 pages • full color • 3rd edition**

Take a Hike in Beautiful Arizona!

Get outdoors with Charles Liu as he helps you find and enjoy the top hikes within 60 miles of the city. These selected trails transport you to scenic overlooks, wildlife hot spots, ancient ruins, and petroglyphs that renew your spirit and recharge your body. Each hike description features key at-a-glance information on distance, difficulty, scenery, traffic, hiking time, and more, so you can quickly learn about the trail. Detailed directions, GPS-based trail maps, and elevation profiles help to ensure that you know where you are and where you're going. Tips on nearby activities further enhance your enjoyment of every outing.

Five-Star Trails:
Flagstaff and Sedona

Tony Padegimas

**ISBN: 978-0-89732-927-9 • $17.95 • 5 x 8
paperback • 280 pages**

Grab Your Pack, and Let's Hit the Trail!

Five-Star Trails: Flagstaff and Sedona presents the best hiking experiences in and around Sedona and Flagstaff: low desert to high peaks, staggering open vistas to claustrophobic canyons, easy to all day. Author Tony Padegimas introduces you to discoveries, surprises, and imaginative ways to explore the geographic area. Each hike features an individual trail map, elevation profile, and at-a-glance information to quickly find the perfect trip. Sized to fit in a pocket, the book's detailed trail descriptions will help you find your way on and off the trail.

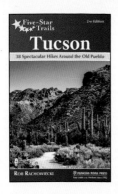

Five-Star Trails: Tucson
Rob Rachowiecki

ISBN: 978-1-63404-100-3 • $17.95 • 5 x 8
paperback • 288 pages • 2nd edition

Explore the Best Trails in Tucson, Arizona!

Tucson is an absolute hiker's nirvana. Bag a peak, or take a dip in a swimming hole. Immerse yourself in the region's American Indian history, or wander among towering rock formations. Hundreds of trails provide endless opportunities to explore. With the expert guidance of Rob Rachowiecki, you'll experience 38 five-star hiking trails, for all levels and interests, divided into six distinct areas. With ratings for scenery, difficulty, trail condition, solitude, and accessibility for children, you can find your perfect outings with just a glance. GPS-based trail maps, elevation profiles, and detailed directions to trailheads help to ensure that you always know where you are and where to go.

Explore Tucson Outdoors: Hiking, Biking, & More
Karen Krebbs

ISBN: 978-1-63404-118-8 • $9.95 • 4.25 x 7.5
spiral bound • 26 pages • full color

The Best of Tucson!

Explore Tucson Outdoors offers the details you need to easily find 20 of the Arizona city's top outdoor locations and a wide variety of activities, including trails in botanical gardens, wetlands, canyons, and forests. The trails are split between walks in the city and hikes in Tucson's wild backyard, so you can enjoy outings in places like nearby Saguaro National Park, the Santa Catalina Mountains, and Tucson Mountain Park. The full-color guide's pocket-sized format is great for a backpack or back pocket, and every site description includes maps, color photos, and directions. Written by local author and naturalist Karen Krebbs, this is your guide to enjoying Tucson in the best possible way: outdoors!

About the Author

Photo: Deborah Crane

LEIGH WILSON is an Illinois native from a family of travelers who sparked a severe case of wanderlust that persists to this day. After living in Iowa, Seattle, and Chicago, she left a corporate marketing career to pursue travel writing in 2017 and now calls Tucson, Arizona, home.

Leigh writes about her travels online at **Campfires & Concierges** (campfiresandconcierges.com) and is a regular contributor to several other travel blogs. She and her Airedale terrier, Bailey, have spent months on the road exploring the western United States, always in search of the next hometown!